IT'S SO MAGIC

LYNDA BARRY

HarperPerennial

A Division of HarperCollinsPublishers

FOR JOHN DONOVAN MULLEN
MY BEST FRIEND IN THE WORLD

MY FISH-BOWL

UN-NATURAL SEL-EC-TION

MARLYS MAYBONNE

Design by Tom Greensfelder in Chicago, ILLINOIS Edited by Tom Greensfalder and John Mullen. Special Thanks to THE RAGDALE FOUNDATION, Lake Forest, ILLINOIS
Matt Groening is FUNKLORD OF U.S.A. Preserve our Prairies. Make Love not Malls. Kevin Kawula drives a big white truck.

FIRST EDITION LIBRARY OF CONGRESS CATALOG CARD NUMBER 93-42053
ISBN 0-06-095046-3 94 95 96 97 98 10 9 8 7 6 5 4 3 2 1

FAMILY PICTURES

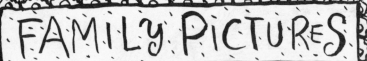

BY LYNDA "I ♡ THERAPY!!!!" BARRY © 1993

AT SCHOOL AT SELMER JR HIGH SCHOOL IN HEALTH A PSYCHOLOGICAL WOMAN CAME IN TO DO EXPERIMENTAL TESTS ON OUR LIVES. OUR ASSIGNMENT: DRAW A PICTURE OF EVERYONE IN YOUR FAMILY DOING SOMETHING. WHAT IF YOU ARE A CRUDDY DRAWER? IT DOES NOT MATTER.

MY SISTER MARLYS
STANDING ON THE CLOSED TOILET SEAT SO SHE CAN WATCH HERSELF SING IN THE MIRROR.

I'M HENERY THE 8TH I AM!

MARLYS. OPEN THIS DAMN DOOR!

I RAISED MY HAND I SAID WHAT SHOULD THEY BE DOING?

MY BROTHER FREDDIE
HE DOESN'T LIVE WITH US I HAVEN'T SEEN HIM IN A LONG TIME BUT HE LOVES INSECTS THIS IS HIM SINGING AT THE FUNERAL OF A FLY.

P.S. I LOVE YOU
YOU, YOU, YOU
YOU, YOU, YOU
I LOVE YOU

THE PSYCHOLOGICAL LADY SAID THEY SHOULD DO WHAT THEY DO NORMALLY

MY MOM. WE DON'T LIVE WITH HER FOR SHE IS TOO HIGH STRUNG. THIS IS HER SHOUTING HOW SHE HATES THE SINGING OF JAMES TAYLOR

FIRE AND RAIN?!? GOOD GOD!!! WHY DO YOU BUY THIS GARBAGE! HE SOUNDS DEAD!!!

6

I RAISED MY HAND I GO WHAT'S THIS FOR?

MY DAD. NO ONE KNOWS WHERE HE'S AT. HE TAKES OFF. THIS IS HIM SINGING WITH THE RADIO IN HIS CAR GOING 80 M.P.H.

♪ DANG ME — DANG ME ♪ THEY OUGHTA TAKE A ROPE AND HANG ME ♪

SHE SAID COULD I PLEASE JUST COMPLETE THE ASSIGNMENT?

MY GRANDMA IF IT WASN'T FOR HER ME AND MY SISTER WOULD BE SCREWED. THIS IS HER IN MASS SINGING. SHE LETS US LIVE WITH HER.

♪ O COME ♪ O COME EE-MAH AH-HAN YOU-EL ♪

I HANDED MY PAPERS TO THE LADY AND SAT DOWN. SHE CALLED MY NAME. COULD SHE EXPLAIN THE PROBLEMS OF MY LIFE? SHE LOOKED AT MY PICTURES FOR A LONG TIME AND THEN SHE LOOKED UP. SHE SAID "WELL MAYBONNE YOU CERTAINLY COME FROM A MUSICAL FAMILY!!!"

ME. MAYBONNE MAYDELLE MULLEN. CAPRICORN. SPAZMO. HATER OF WAR, PREJUDICE AND POLLUTION. ME LAYING IN MY BED IN THE MIDDLE OF THE NIGHT LISTENING TO THREE DOG NIGHT ON MY CLOCK RADIO AND THE SOUND OF MY SISTER MARLYS BREATHING, WAITING FOR MY LIFE TO COME TRUE.

♪ ONE IS THE LONLIEST NUMBAH ♪ ONE IS THE LONLIEST NUMBAH

7

MORE BEAUTIFUL

BY LYNDA "WATCH THAT MONKEY" BARRY © 1991

WHEN YOU'RE CLOSE TO ME I CAN FEEL YOUR HEARTBEAT I CAN HEAR YOU BREATHING IN MY EAR. MY SISTER SINGS IT WITH THE RADIO. THE SONG "GROOVY KIND OF LOVE" SHE SAYS SHE NEVER HEARD A SONG MORE BEAUTIFUL.

SHE SAYS SHE WANTS GROOVY LOVE IN HER LIFE. I SAY "SAME HERE" THE SUN IS COMING THROUGH THE KITCHEN WINDOW AND SHE LAYS HER HEAD IN THE LIT UP SQUARE ON THE TABLE AND CLOSES HER EYES. HER MOUTH MOVES ON THE SONG WORDS THEN SHE TELLS ME THE SECRET OF THERE'S SOMEONE SHE LIKES. I SAY WHAT'S HIS NAME. SHE SAYS KEVIN TURNER

8

HE SITS IN ROW THREE AND SHE KNOWS THE BACK OF HIS HEAD BY HEART. SHE ASKED THE MAGIC EIGHT BALL DID HE LIKE HER ALSO AND IT SAID ASK AGAIN LATER. SHE SAID SHE SPIT ON A GUY FOR CALLING HIM KEVIN TURKEY AND THE GUY SLUGGED HER BUT THE SLUG WAS WORTH IT. SHE SAYS KEVIN SMELLS LIKE MOTHBALLS AND NOW MOTHBALLS SMELL LIKE FLOWERS.

OUTSIDE IN THE GARDEN THERE'S PLANTS COMING UP AND MORE BIRDS SITTING ON THE CLOTHES POLE. "KEVIN RAN THE 100 YARD DASH THE FASTEST OF ANYONE AND HE DIDN'T ACT CONCEITED WOULDN'T YOU AGREE BABY YOU AND ME GOT A GROOVY KIND OF LOVE." SHE SINGS IT TO HIM WITH HER EYES SHUT TIGHT. KEVIN TURNER CAN YOU HEAR IT?

9

ALL DIFFERENT

BY LYNDA "HONESTYVILLE" BARRY © 1991

HAVE YOU EVER WATCHED SOMEONE FALL IN LOVE? HOW THEY TURN ALL DIFFERENT? THAT'S MY SISTER MARLYS. RIGHT NOW SHE'S MAKING KISSING NOISES TO MR. LUDERMYER'S DOG.

YOU NOTICE HOW NO MATTER WHAT YOU SAY TO THEM THEY KEEP BEING HAPPY? THIS MORNING I BURNED THE PANCAKES. MARLYS SAID THEY NEVER TASTED BETTER. I SUCKED THE HEAD OF HER BARBIE UP THE VACUUM CLEANER. SHE SAID SHE ALWAYS HATED THAT DOLL.

RIGHT NOW SHE IS LOVING ALL MUSIC.
EVEN THE SONGS ABOUT STOMACH
RELIEF. AND ALL THINGS LOOK BEAU-
TIFUL TO HER INCLUDING LINT BALLS
AND MEAT BALLS AND OLD GUM IN
THE STREET.

OUR FATHER WHO ART IN HEAVEN
IT'S HER FIRST TIME AND SHE
DOESN'T KNOW THAT FEELING GOES
AWAY. SO PLEASE FATHER, IN ALL
YOUR MERCIFUL WISDOM, COULD YOU
PLEASE JUST KEEP YOUR MOUTH SHUT
A LITTLE LONGER?

WHY·DID·HE?

BY LYNDA BARRY WITH LAUREN GAFFNEY © 1991

THE BOY NAMED KEVIN TURNER WHO MARLYS LOVES, LOVES HER BACK. MARLYS SAYS SHE KNOWS HE LOVES HER BACK OR ELSE WHY DID HE WAIT FOR HER EVERY DAY BY ROOM 4 SAYING "HI MARLYS. HI TWINKIE."

TWINKIE BECAUSE MARLYS ALWAYS SPLIT HER PACKAGE WITH HIM. SHE HAS WIPED OUT ALL THE MONEY IN HER ABRAHAM LINCOLN HEAD BANK BUYING TWINKIES TO SPLIT WITH KEVIN TURNER. KEVIN TURNER, KEVIN TURNER. SHE HAS SAID HIS NAME 100 TIMES FAST WITH HER EYES CLOSED TIGHT.

12

MARLYS SAYS SHE KNOWS HE LOVES HER BACK EVEN THOUGH AROUND HIS FRIENDS HE ACTED DIFFERENT. TODAY AROUND HIS FRIENDS HE SAID THE SAME NAME FOR HER, TWINKIE, ONLY SHOUTING IT NOW AND LAUGHING. TWINKIE AND SOME OTHER WORDS AND MARLYS SAYS IT'S NO BIG DEAL.

NO BIG DEAL, SHE SAYS, THEN LOOKS DOWN AND STOPS TALKING. AND FOR THE FIRST TIME I EVER SAW, SHE'S QUIET. JUST QUIET AND STARING DOWN WITHOUT MOVING.

CALLING OUT FOR LOVE

story idea By Susie Esbejornson • Draws by LYNDA BARRY 1991 ©

Where do dreams come from? <u>Number one:</u> your imaginations. <u>Number two:</u> could be a secret power of e.s.p. trying to tell you something! This is my dream I was playing with some friends by the Black Lagoon.

marlys you were right this place is great!

marlys its another perfect idea you had!

I was looking like a queen

Thank you royal subjects!

Suddenly with no warning!

notice I'm not even scared

Its the creature run for it man!

run marlys for your life!

ARRRR ARRRR

The Creature OF THE BLACK LAGOON!

ARRR

ARRRR!

ARRRR!

Sorry I cannot understand your message!

CAN I HELP You?

I AM MARLYS.

14

for a long time the creature made noises and I tried to understand what was the problem. Finally I guessed it right!

You feel embarrassed because you look so dirty!

ARRRRR!!

ARRR!!

Don't worry at all!

That's OK I will clean you off!

Turns out the best thing to clean the creature with is school paper towels. I GOT A BUNCH.

I am coming!

ARRRRR!

I wiped off the creature until he was clean. He felt so beautiful and happy.

your welcome creature but I'm sorry but I cannot be your girlfriend.

Arrr

ARRR

What?

yes I will help you find a girlfriend

I like you only as a friend.

I tried to see if my sister would be the creatures girlfriend but she was too stuck up for him. Then I woke up. What was the message of my dream? Sometimes a monster can be Great! Sometimes a monster can be doing a love call to you. The End? by Marlys

15

IF·YOU·CAN·BELIEVE·IT

by LYNDA "EL HOSEMASTER" BARRY © 1991

DON'T EVER ASK A GUY IF HE LIKES YOU, THAT'S THE NUMBER ONE THING YOU CAN DO TO WRECK YOUR CHANCES, I TRIED TO TELL MARLYS BUT SHE JUST LOOKED AT ME AND KEPT WRITING: "DEAR KEVIN, TRUTH OR DARE"

MR. Gasser

"TRUTH IS: TELL ME DO YOU LIKE ME. DARE IS: I DARE YOU TO TELL ME DO YOU LIKE ME." YOU DON'T KNOW BOYS I TELL HER BUT SHE GIVES HIM THE LETTER ANYWAY WITH A PERFECT DRAWING ON IT OF A DADDY ROTH RACE CAR. KEVIN'S FAVORITE. "ART IS GOOD FOR THINGS" SHE SAYS.

Mothers worry

IF YOU CAN BELIEVE IT THE ANSWER OF KEVIN IS YES. YES HE LIKES MARLYS BUT ITS A LET'S MAKE A DEAL. DOOR NUMBER ONE IS SHE HAS TO KEEP IT SECRET. DOOR NUMBER TWO IS SHE HAS TO KEEP MAKING HIM DRAWINGS. AND DOOR NUMBER THREE IS HE GETS TO TELL PEOPLE IT WAS HIM WHO MADE THE DRAWINGS.

WORTH IT! SHOUTS MARLYS. WORTH IT WORTH IT WORTH IT TO THE MILLIONTH POWER! YOU CAN SEE HER RIGHT NOW BENDING OVER THE PAPER AND DRAWING. SNEAKING OUT OF BED AT NIGHT AND DRAWING THE PICTURES FOR KEVIN TURNER ALWAYS LEAVING THE PERFECT SPOT EMPTY FOR WHERE HE CAN SIGN HIS NAME.

SO THEY TRADE

by LYNDA "NOT THE MONEY" BARRY ☺♡☺ ©1991

I SAID TO MARLYS IF KEVIN REALLY LIKES YOU THEN WHY DOES HE SAY YOU CAN'T TELL, WHY DOES HE MAKE YOU KEEP DRAWING HIM DRAGSTERS, AND WHY DOES HE KEEP SAYING IT WAS HIM WHO MADE THOSE DRAWINGS? I TOLD HER THAT'S NOT LIKING, THAT'S USING.

I TOLD HER I KNOW GUYS AND I KNOW THEIR SPAZZY ACTIONS AND SHE SAID IF I DIDN'T MIND IT COULD I PLEASE JUST SHUT UP? I SAID DON'T YOU GET IT? THIS IS ADVICE, AND SHE SAID NO YOU'RE THE ONE WHO'S NOT GETTING IT. OH YEAH? I SAY. OH YEAH? THEN SHE TELLS ME.

18

NUMBER ONE: KEVIN SAYS DON'T TELL BECAUSE OF THE GIRL ALICE BULZOMI WHO ALSO LOVES HIM AND ALICE IS BIG AND WILL KICK MARLYS WITH HER POINTED SHOES AND ALSO KEVIN IF SHE EVER FINDS OUT. NUMBER TWO: MARLYS DRAWS HIM DRAGSTERS BECAUSE KEVIN LOVES DRAGSTERS BUT TRAGICALLY HE IS A CRUDDY DRAWER OF DRAGSTERS. THAT IS JUST LIFE MARLYS SAYS.

WHAT HE'S GOOD AT DRAWING IS NATURE AND FLOWERS. SO THEY TRADE. THEN MARLYS SHOWS ME THE STACK OF SECRET DRAWINGS HE MADE HER. TWENTY SEVEN DRAWINGS IN A PAY 'N' SAVE BAG WITH THE PENCIL HANDWRITING ON THE TOP:

To Marlys your the greatest girl artist of dragsters from Kevin.

PENCIL HANDWRITING SHE TRACES WITH HER FINGER, THEN SHE LOOKS AT ME AND SMILES.

The MARLYS NEWSPAPER!!!

by LYNDA: GOODBYE SEAN COLLINS BARRY © 1991

the #1 reporter!

Please read Marlys newspaper! It is a great newspaper for all your information!

Price? It is free for my friends

Weather today it will be great!!

KEVIN TURNER LOSES HIS OTHER TOOTH!!

IT WAS HERE
THIS DOES NOT LOOK LIKE HIM THAT MUCH.

Last night he was eating a sucker called <u>Black Cow</u> and it came out. The first tooth he lost still has not grown in. Kevin is in stable condition he got 25¢ under his pillow other things are everywhere else

Marlys SETS RECORD on eating MARI SHINO CHERRIES!

On monday marlys bought a full jar of marishino cherries from A+P with <u>her own</u> money. One by one she ate them 47 cherries!! She had a comment: They are so delicious!! She drank grape pop to go with it!

ADVICE OF MARLYS by marlys!

Dear Marlys. I think you are incredible on advice. here's my problem. A person whose name I won't say is looking inside peoples lunch boxes everyday but he just tells the teacher I have to get something in my coat. She always lets him in the coat room. Then he goes all in your lunch box and moves around your sandwhich what should I do? signed "Mysterious."

Dear Mysterious Know what I would do is write a note in my lunch box with that guys name on it. Write "I know you are doing

→ This! so quit it!

COMICS
NORMAN the CAT
by Kevin turner

1) how many times I tell you norman don't play with matches!

2) norman thats real dynamite not a toy, oh NO!

3) KABLOOOEY

4) oh good it was just a dream

THE END??

SPORTS

Tumbeling Class after school in Mrs. Allen's. Rm 9.

Please join our tumbeling class in Mrs. Allen's room, room 9. We use mats and music you can bring your own records. You will learn gracefullness. Its not just for girls!! (come on to tumbeling! Marlys did the record on backwards summer saulting. 27 could have done more except she hit a desk and had to relax.

4th Graders Clobber 5th Graders in Lunch Kickball Game!!! IT was so Great!!!

WE won it!
gay
gay
you cheated
sore loser

The 4th graders won at lunch Kickball. Theres people saying we cheated because they're sore losers. Just ignore them! Victory is ours!!!

MOVIES

In mrs. allens we saw a filmstrip From Larva to butterfly. It was Incredible !! Only one person FELL ASLEEP during the show!!!!!!!!!!!!!!!!

PETS

HAMPSTER CROAKS IN MRS. BRYANTS!! BY Anonomys!!

mona

Look shes dead
oh no
People crying

Go back to your seats!
mrs. Bryant

MONA
our Grave for Mona

mona the hampster in Mrs. Bryants is dead. One guy in the class said the name of the desease that Killed mona is a famous desease of hampsters called The Big Butt Desease. (Please don't laugh its tragic) People said lets bury her at least But Mrs Bryant said I'll take care of it and later someone saw her put Mona in the Janitors Garbage! Cold blooded Award #1 Goes to Mrs Bryant but lucky thing we Got Mona out + Buried Her!

JIM COMING SLOWLY

This story by Ruth Williamson. Drawings by Lynda Barry ©1991

THE PHONE RANG, KEVIN TURNER ASKING FOR MARLYS. HANG ON I SAY. IT'S AN EMERGENCY HE SAYS. THEN IT'S MARLYS WALKING IN MY ROOM SAYING SHE HAS TO GO TO KEVIN'S AND I HAVE TO TAKE HER BECAUSE IT'S TOO FAR AND GRANDMA WON'T LET HER WALK BY HERSELF. "IT WILL BE WORTH IT TO YOU" SHE SAYS.

NOR

TURNS OUT KEVIN HAS AN AUNT NAMED AUNT MARY AND AUNT MARY HAS A BIRD NAMED JIM, AND ALL OF THEM WERE SITTING AROUND THE KITCHEN, AND AUNT MARY WAS SHOWING KEVIN JIM'S FAMOUS TRICK OF THE UPSIDE DOWN HANG ON HER FINGER AND JIM SHOWED AUNT MARY HIS OTHER FAMOUS TRICK OF NOW I WILL FLY BEHIND THE REFRIGERATOR.

FOR ONE HOUR STRAIGHT AUNT MARY WAS BENT BY THE REFRIGERATOR GOING JIM JIM JIM JIM JIM. THEN KEVIN CALLED MARLYS BECAUSE HE KNOWS SHE IS GOOD WITH ANIMALS. WHEN WE GOT THERE AUNT MARY WAS SMOKING CIGARETTES AND SAYING "I JUST CANNOT TAKE IT ANYMORE" SHE WOULDN'T LET US MOVE THE REFRIGERATOR BECAUSE IF JIM WAS LOCATED WRONG IT COULD HAVE A TRAGIC EFFECT.

MARLYS'S IDEA WAS TO LAY ON TOP OF THE REFRIGERATOR AND SING "BORN FREE" DOWN THE CRACK. KEVIN SAID IF SHE WANTED HE WOULD DO IT TOO, THEN ALL YOU SAW WAS THEIR FEET STICKING OFF THE EDGE AND THEN THE SOUND OF THEIR VOICES AND AUNT MARY'S HUSBAND WALKS IN AND SAYS "CHRIST." THEN THE MIRACLE. THE WALKING DUSTBALL OF JIM COMING SLOWLY ONTO THE LINOLEUM. "HE'S ALIVE!!" SHOUTS AUNT MARY. "JIM IS ALIVE!!"

ALL THE ALL

DRAW LYNDA "TWINS WIN!!" BARRY © 1991
WILLIAM SHAKESPEARE WROTE IT. SONNET XXXI

THY BOSOM IS ENDEARED WITH ALL HEARTS WHICH I BY LACKING HAVE SUPPOSED DEAD; AND THERE REIGNS LOVE, AND ALL LOVE'S LOVING PARTS, AND ALL THOSE FRIENDS WHICH I THOUGHT BURIED.

HOW MANY A HOLY AND OBSEQUIOUS TEAR HATH DEAR RELIGIOUS LOVE STOL'N FROM MINE EYE, AS INTEREST OF THE DEAD, WHICH NOW APPEAR BUT THINGS REMOV'D THAT HIDDEN IN THEE LIE!

THOU ART THE GRAVE WHERE BURIED LOVE DOTH LIVE, HUNG WITH THE TROPHIES OF MY LOVERS GONE, WHO ALL THEIR PARTS OF ME TO THEE DID GIVE: THAT DUE OF MANY NOW IS THINE ALONE.

EXCUSE ME AHEM EXCUSE ME BUT THERE'S SOMEONE BEHIND YOU.

THEIR IMAGES I LOVED I VIEW IN THEE, AND THOU (ALL THEY) HAST ALL THE ALL OF ME.

25

HOW TO GROOVE ON LIFE

BY LYNDA "DO YOU DYE YOUR HAIR?" BARRY ©1991

OF COURSE BY MARLYS!!

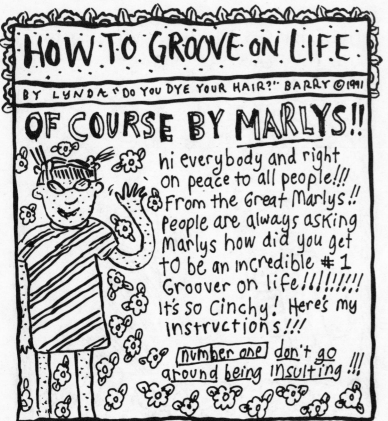

hi everybody and right on peace to all people!!! From the Great Marlys!! people are always asking Marlys how did you get to be an incredible #1 Groover on life!!!!!!!!!! It's so Cinchy! Here's my instructions!!!

Number one don't go around being insulting!!!

number two Be Kind to animals for it is hard to Groove on life when they are biting you!!!

Here Boy

Have some poison baloney

Wrong

ow wait wait it was just a joke!

LATER on

NUMBER 3 Don't hog everything!!!!

Everything in the world that's decent is mine!!
Then why don't You share it!!!
Because why should I?
So You won't be so cruddy
That is incredible adivice!!

NUMBER four Fix your hair all Gorgeous! and fix other peoples hair all gorgeous!!!

EXCUSE ME

do you like it? it is Gorgeous Created by marlys! She's incredible!

PLEASE I must have her phone number

S·T·A·R·T· YE·L·L·I·N·G

By LYNDA "PASS ME MR. CRAWDADDY" BARRY © 1991

WE WOKE UP AND HE WAS BACK. HIM SLEEPING ON THE COUCH. OUR UNCLE JOHN SNORING LOUD IN THE FRONT ROOM AND GRANDMA SAYING "NOW YOU KIDS DON'T WAKE HIM UP CHRIST I THINK HE DROVE THE 27 HOURS STRAIGHT THROUGH."

LOOK OUT THE WINDOW AND SEE HIS BLUE CAR. THE 4,000 BUGS CREAMED ONTO THE FRONT AND MARLYS COMES IN RUNNING WITH AN ORANGE AND BLACK WING "IT WAS JUST STUCK THERE STILL PERFECT!" SHE TELLS ME PLEASE HELP HER TAPE IT TO AN INDEX CARD SO WHEN UNCLE JOHN WAKES UP HE WILL ALREADY HAVE A SOUVENIR.

30

MARLYS TAPING STRIPES OF TAPE ACROSS THE WING THEN GETTING THE IDEA TO TAPE MORE BUGS INTO AN ARRANGEMENT. HER OUT THERE BENDING BY THE HEADLIGHT LOOKING FOR THE BEST ONES TO TAPE AROUND RED EL MARKO WORDS "WELCOME BACK THE GREAT UNCLE JOHN!" AND MY GRANDMA SEEING IT AND SAYING "OH FOR THE LOVE OF GOD."

Welcome back the GREAT UNCLE John!

US WAITING AND WAITING FOR HIM TO WAKE UP. IF YOU EVER KNEW HIM YOU WOULD KNOW WHY. WE NEVER KNEW ANYONE AS GREAT OR INTER- ESTING. THAT IS WHY MARLYS FIN- ALLY HAD TO JUST RUN INTO THE LIVING ROOM AND START YELLING "SURPRISE!"

TAKE A PICTURE

BY LYNDA "SHUCK THEM OYSTERS" BARRY • NEWORLEANS © 1991

"HE IS MY ROOFTOP." IT'S A SONG ABOUT JESUS THAT I HEARD ONCE IN CHURCH. IT'S SUNDAY MORNING AND GRANDMA IS GETTING HER HAIR READY FOR MASS. BUT NOT US. WE'RE GOING FISHING WITH MY UNCLE JOHN.

MARLYS WALKS IN ALL DRESSED UP. "YOU CHANGED YOUR MIND." GRANDMA SAYS. BUT NO. MARLYS IS DRESSED UP FOR UNCLE JOHN. HIM AND THE FISH. OUR GRANDMA SHUTS THE FRONT DOOR AND WE WATCH HER WALK DOWN THE STREET. "SHE'S MAD AT US" I SAY. "WORTH IT." SAYS MARLYS. WE HAVEN'T BEEN FISHING SINCE WE LAST SAW OUR DAD.

"YOU STILL HAVEN'T GOT MARRIED?" SAYS MARLYS. WE'RE IN THE CAR DRIVING. "HELL NO!" SAYS UNCLE JOHN. "HELL NO!" SAYS MARLYS. YOU KNOW THAT BROTHERS CAN LOOK ALIKE AND UNCLE JOHN'S MY DAD'S. FROM A SIDEWAYS VIEW I CAN SEE HIM. SEE MY DAD'S FACE MOVING THERE AND I DON'T EVEN KNOW HOW.

"WHY DON'T YOU TAKE A PICTURE IT LASTS LONGER." UNCLE JOHN'S USUAL COMMENT WHEN HE SEES ME STARING. THEN HIM LAUGHING NOT MEAN AND TOUCHING MY SHOULDER. "YEAH" SAYS MARLYS BUT WHEN I LOOK AT HER SHE'S STARING TOO. STARING AT HIM DRIVING WITH HIS HANDS ON THE STEERING WHEEL. I MEAN HOW CAN YOU HELP IT?

YOU CALL ELAINE

BY LYNDA EL PASO BARRY ✿ ✿ ✿ © 1991

MY UNCLE JOHN PUTS SPAGHETTI IN HIS MOUTH. MY GRANDMA WATCHES HIM EAT. "YOU EVER HEAR FROM THAT LOIS BA-RIGI? NOW SHE WAS A PRETTY ONE." MY UNCLE SHAKES HIS HEAD NO. "SHE WAS SO CRAZY ABOUT YOU, JOHNNY." MY UNCLE KEEPS EATING.

"YOU GOING TO LOOK UP ELAINE WHILE YOU'RE IN TOWN?" MY GRANDMA SAYS. "I KNOW SHE'S JUST DYING TO HEAR FROM YOU. DIVORCED NOW YOU KNOW."

"I KNOW." SAYS UNCLE JOHN.

"WELL, I ALWAYS USED TO SAY SHE MISSED HER CHANCE WITH YOU JOHNNY. MARLYS GO GET MY CIGARETTES FOR ME HONEY."

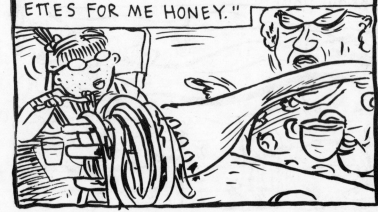

"HOW'S YOUR ARTHRITIS, MA?" UNCLE JOHN DOESN'T LOOK UP WHEN HE SAYS IT. "NOW JOHNNY, ELAINE WOULD BE SO TICKLED IF YOU CALLED HER. MARLYS GO GET GRANDMA'S HAND BAG I GOT ELAINE'S NUMBER ON THE CHURCH PROGRAM." UNCLE JOHN WIPES HIS MOUTH AND STANDS UP. "WHY THE FACE?" MY GRANDMA SAYS. "WE'RE JUST TALKING." MY UNCLE PULLS OUT HIS KEYS.

"YOU'RE NOT GOING OUT WITH THAT BILL AGAIN TONIGHT JOHNNY." MY GRANDMA STANDS UP. "WHY?" MY SISTER SAYS. "WE LIKE BILL." SHE HANDS GRANDMA HER PURSE AND MY GRANDMA HANDS MY UNCLE THE PAPER WITH THE NUMBER AND HE WON'T TAKE IT. "WHY? YOU GOT A GIRL I DON'T KNOW ABOUT, DON'T YOU?" "NO" SAYS MY UNCLE. MY GRANDMA POINTS TO THE PAPER ON THE TABLE. "YOU CALL ELAINE."

Watch. It. There.

BY LYNDA BARRY © 1991

"OK EVERYBODY, PILE IN!" MY UNCLE JOHN GETS IN THE CAR. TONIGHT WE'RE GOING TO THE DRIVE-IN. ME, CINDY LUDERMYER, MARLYS AND KEVIN TURNER. "DON'T LET THEM EAT JUNK!" MY GRANDMA SHOUTS BUT WE ARE ALREADY DRIVING AWAY.

FIRST STOP IS TO PICK UP UNCLE JOHN'S FRIEND BILL. BILL WITH THE ALL GOLD FILLINGS. ASK HIM TO SHOW YOU AND HE'LL OPEN HIS MOUTH ANYTIME. HE RUNS TO THE CAR WITH TWO GIANT BROWN BAGS OF POPCORN. "HELLO EVERYBODY!" "THAT COLOGNE!" UNCLE JOHN SAYS. "JESUS, BILL!" WE ROLL DOWN THE WINDOWS.

36

THE MOVIE IS A DOUBLE FEATURE TARZAN. IN THE CAR LINE KEVIN SAYS HE HAD AN UNCLE THAT WAS TARZAN ONCE. IT WAS IN A T.V. COMMERCIAL FOR APPLIANCES WHERE HE JUMPED ON A WASHER AND SHOUTED ABOUT THE VALUES. "UP FRONT OR IN BACK?" UNCLE JOHN SAYS DRIVING BY THE SPEAKER POSTS. WE SAY FRONT! FRONT!

IT'S JUST STARTING TO GET DARK. MARLYS AND KEVIN TURNER PUT A BLANKET ON THE ROOF OF THE CAR TO WATCH IT THERE. ME AND CINDY DO OUR WALK AROUND SEA HUNT FOR CUTE GUYS. AND UNCLE JOHN AND BILL SIT IN THE FRONT SEAT SMOKING AND LAUGHING THEIR HEADS OFF UNTIL THE BEAM OF THE PROJECTOR FINALLY SHOOTS ON AND THE MOVIES BEGIN.

YOU KNEW

BY LYNDA "GO NORTHSTARS!" BARRY © 1991

WE'RE IN LINE TO BUY COKES. ME AND CINDY LUDERMYER AT THE DRIVE-IN AND THE MOVIE IS STARTING AND I WATCH HER TALKING TO ME AND I WATCH TARZAN JUMP FROM A TREE AND SWING BEHIND HER HEAD ON A VINE WHILE SHE ASKS ME IF IT'S WEIRD THAT MY UNCLE'S A QUEER.

IN THE CAR MY UNCLE SITS WITH HIS FRIEND BILL, I CAN SEE THE SHADOWS OF THEIR HEADS MOVING LAUGHING. "BILL'S FOR SURE A KNOWN QUEER" CINDY SAYS, PEELING HER STRAW, THEN SHE TELLS ME SHE FELT SORRY FOR HIM, ALL THOSE GUYS KICKING HIS ASS THAT NIGHT BEHIND DUMAINES. TARZAN RUNS YELLING ACROSS THE JUNGLE FLOOR.

"NOT THAT I THINK YOU ARE WEIRD FOR HAVING A QUEER UNCLE" SAYS CINDY. WE'RE WALKING BACK TO THE CAR ME HOLDING THE CARDBOARD TRAY OF COKES FOR MARLYS, KEVIN, BILL AND UNCLE JOHN. HOW CAN IT BE THAT YOU CAN KNOW SOMETHING YOU NEVER KNEW YOU KNEW UNTIL SOMEONE SAYS IT? MARLYS SINGS FROM THE ROOF OF THE CAR WHEN SHE SEES US:

"TARZAN THE MONKEY MAN BROKE HIS ARM ON A RUBBER BAND!" I HAND UP TWO COKES, THEN TWO IN THE WINDOWS TO UNCLE JOHN AND BILL. UNCLE JOHN AND BILL. UNCLE JOHN AND BILL. THEN IT'S ME AND CINDY WALKING AGAIN. "HOW COME YOU'RE NOT TALKING?" SHE SAYS. I GO, "I'M TALKING." "DON'T WORRY" SHE SAYS. "IT'S NOT LIKE I'M GOING TO TELL ANYBODY."

39

ON PURPOSE

By LYNDA LA BREA TAR PIT BARRY © 1991

ACCORDING TO CINDY LUDERMYER MY UNCLE JOHN IS AN ACTUAL QUEER WITH HIS FRIEND BILL. AT THE DRIVE IN WE WATCHED THEM WITH THE POPCORN. ONE BOX THEY SHARED AND LAUGHING FOR NO REASON AT PARTS OF TARZAN IN THE VALLEY OF GOLD.

CINDY SAID NO MATTER WHAT DON'T LET MARLYS EVER KNOW ABOUT THE QUEERNESS OF UNCLE JOHN. IT COULD DO SOMETHING TO HER. I SAY "LIKE WHAT?" AND CINDY LOOKS AT ME LIKE I AM SO STUPID. MARLYS AND KEVIN KONKED OUT ON THE BLANKET WHEN THE MOVIE SAYS "THE END" AND THE STARS ABOVE ARE SHINING. O HOLY NIGHT JESUS DID YOU MAKE QUEERS ON PURPOSE?

THE END

UNCLE JOHN LIFTS MARLYS AND BILL LIFTS KEVIN BOTH SLEEPING AND CINDY HITS MY ARM "THEY SHOULDN'T BE TOUCHING THEM" SHE WHISPERS. CINDY LUDERMYER SOMETIMES I WISH YOU WOULD JUST BLOW UP. EXPLODE INTO A MILLION PIECES STARTING WITH YOUR MOUTH. UNCLE JOHN STARTS THE CAR. TOMORROW AT SCHOOL EVERYONE WILL KNOW.

DEAR HEAVENLY FATHER I WILL GIVE YOU ONE MILLION DOLLARS TO TAKE BILL'S ARM OFF THE BACK OF THE FRONT SEAT HIS HAND ONE INCH FROM UNCLE JOHN AND CINDY'S EYES LIKE SCIENCE CLASS MICRO-SCOPES. I LEAN FORWARD. "BILL'S HOUSE IS CLOSER" I SAY. "DROP HIM OFF FIRST." UNCLE JOHN TURNS HIS HEAD AROUND AND HE LOOKS STRAIGHT AT ME. "DROP HIM OFF FIRST." I SAY AGAIN.

HAPPIEST THING

BY LYNDA "CHICAGO BULLS" BARRY © 1991

CAN AN UNCLE STILL BE YOUR FAVORITE UNCLE EVEN IF HE'S QUEER? I SAY YES LOGICALLY BUT RIGHT NOW I SAY IT SECRETLY. THANK YOU CINDY LUDERMYER FOR TELLING THE WHOLE WORLD.

DID YOU EVER HAVE A BEST FRIEND YOU DON'T EVEN KNOW WHY YOU LIKE? CINDY SAYS ONE PROOF OF QUEERS BEING BAD IS JESUS IS AGAINST QUEERS. I SAID "HOW SHOULD YOU KNOW?" SHE SAID "THE BIBLE." I SAID "WHERE IN THE BIBLE?" SHE IS STILL LOOKING. SHE IS STILL LOOKING FOR WHERE JESUS BROKE THE NEWS ABOUT QUEERS.

IT'S NOT JUST JESUS AGAINST QUEERS, ACCORDING TO CINDY, IT'S THE AGREEMENT OF THE PEOPLE. I SAID WHAT ABOUT YOU CINDY, ARE YOU AGAINST QUEERS? SHE SAID WHY WAS I SO RACKED UP ABOUT IT? WE WERE UP IN HER BEDROOM. I WAS SUPPOSED TO SPEND THE NIGHT. "I GOT AN IDEA." SHE SAYS.

ON THE CROSS BY HER BED HUNG JESUS WITH HIS EYES CLOSED. CINDY SAID WE COULD DO A PRAYER TO LIFT THE QUEERNESS OUT OF UNCLE JOHN. IN THE NAME OF THE FATHER, THE SON AND THE HOLY GHOST NO DON'T DO IT!!!!! CINDY PRAYED GO AND I PRAYED STOP. WHAT IF THE QUEERNESS IS UNCLE JOHN'S HAPPIEST THING?

THIS PRAYER

BY LYNDA "BULLS WIN!" BARRY ✿ ✿ ©1991

DEAR JESUS SON OF GOD IN HEAVEN IS IT TRUE YOU ARE AGAINST QUEERS? I HAVE BEEN THINKING SO HARD ABOUT THE SUBJECT BECAUSE OF MY FAVORITE UNCLE. UNCLE JOHN. I'M SURE YOU KNOW OF HIM.

SHE'S STILL CRYING. I JUST LOOKED IN HER ROOM AND SHE'S STILL CRYING.

DRINK YOUR MILK.

DON'T BOSS ME

I'M PRETTY SURE WHAT HE HAS WITH BILL IS REAL LOVE BECAUSE HE'S DRIVING BACK TO PORTLAND MONDAY AND HE ASKED BILL TO COME WITH HIM AND BILL SAID YES AND NOW BILL IS HAVING HIS YARD SALE. HE'S MOVING AND EVERYTHING MUST GO. I BOUGHT THIS PEN I AM WRITING YOU WITH FROM BILL.

I DON'T GET WHAT'S WRONG BUT YOU GET WHAT'S WRONG BUT YOU WON'T TELL ME

DRINK IT.

YOU THINK YOU'RE SO BIG.

I ALSO BOUGHT ALL OF BILL'S BREAD ALBUMS. BILL SAID "YOU DON'T HAVE TO PAY ME." I SAID "FORGET THAT, BILL." YOU SHOULD SEE BILL AND UNCLE JOHN THEY ARE SO HAPPY YOU CAN TELL IT'S TRUE LOVE. MY GRANDMA THREW A PLATE ACROSS THE KITCHEN WHEN SHE FOUND OUT BILL WAS GOING SHE SHOUTED YOUR NAME WHEN SHE DID IT. DID YOU HEAR?

IT'S 'CAUSE OF BILL ISN'T IT. 'CAUSE HE GOT ASKED BY UNCLE JOHN TO GO WITH, AND SHE'S CRYING BECAUSE THEY'RE QUEERS.

RIGHT?

EVERYONE EXCEPT ME AND MARLYS IS AGAINST UNCLE JOHN AND BILL RIGHT NOW AND I KNOW MORE THAN MOST PEOPLE YOU KNOW HOW THAT FEELS. GRANDMA THREW UNCLE JOHN'S THINGS IN THE YARD AND TOLD HIM DON'T COME BACK. DEAREST JESUS THIS PRAYER ISN'T FOR UNCLE JOHN AND BILL FOR I THINK THEY WILL BE ALL RIGHT. IT'S FOR HER. IT'S FOR GRANDMA WHO CAN'T SEE THAT YET.

I KNOW I'M RIGHT BECAUSE MR. LUDERMYER SAID IT.

FORGET MR. LUDERMYER.

I WILL IF YOU TELL ME WHAT'S QUEERS.

CATCHING UP

LYNDA "HAIL EL VEZ!" BARRY © 1991

UNCLE JOHN AND BILL ARE GONE. GONE BACK TO PORTLAND THEY DROVE AWAY AT 6AM. IT WAS ME WHO MADE THEM COFFEE. ME WHO SNUCK OUT AT 5:00 TO RUN DOWN THE EMPTY STREETS TO BILL'S SO I COULD SAY GOODBYE AND I TURN AROUND AND SEE MARLYS BEHIND ME CATCHING UP.

IT'S NOT EASY HAVING AN UNCLE THAT'S A QUEER. MAINLY BECAUSE OF OTHER PEOPLE. BUT CAN YOU HELP WHO YOU FALL IN LOVE WITH? THEY WERE LOADING THE CAR WHEN WE GOT THERE AND WHEN I SAW UNCLE JOHN I STARTED CRYING THEN BILL STARTED CRYING. GOD I LIKE BILL. "YOU TWO KNOCK IT OFF." SAYS UNCLE JOHN AND MARLYS SAYS "YOU'RE COMING BACK, RIGHT?"

SHE SAYS, "YOU'RE COMING BACK AT CHRISTMAS, RIGHT?" AND UNCLE JOHN SAYS "BET YOU CAN'T LIFT THIS BOX." "BET I CAN TOO" SHE SAYS, AND WE HELP THEM FINISH LOADING. THAT WAS SEVEN HOURS AGO. I WONDER WHERE THEY ARE BY NOW. HE TOOK US TO DRIVE-INS, HE TOOK US FISHING, HE TAUGHT MARLYS HOW TO DO THE BACKFLOAT.

ARE WE BUSTED?

I DON'T KNOW BUT GRANDMA'S FOR SURE AWAKE.

WHERE DO WE SAY WE WERE?

HELP ME THINK OF SOMETHING.

IN THE MOVIES BY "THE END", PEOPLE ARE SUPPOSED TO UNDERSTAND EACH OTHER. THAT'S WHY I THINK THE MOVIE OF UNCLE JOHN AND MY GRANDMA MUST ONLY BE AT INTERMISSION. SO THERE IS STILL HOPE OF A HAPPY ENDING, IT JUST WON'T BE TODAY. HELLO TO UNCLE JOHN AND BILL WHERE EVER YOU ARE. IF YOU'RE READING THIS RIGHT ON LOVE FROM MAYBONNE AND MARLYS. WE MISS YOU SO BAD.

HI GRANDMA

FOR THE LOVE OF GOD YOU TWO! WHAT ARE YOU DOING OUTSIDE AT THIS HOUR?

ENJOYING LIFE. YOU KNOW, JUST GOOFING AROUND.

MARLYS' GUIDE to QUEERS

by LYNDA "SEAN COLLINS" BARRY © 1991

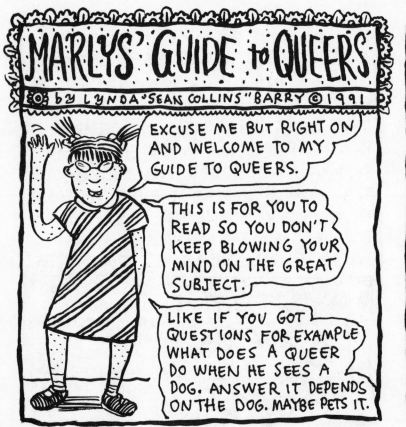

EXCUSE ME BUT RIGHT ON AND WELCOME TO MY GUIDE TO QUEERS.

THIS IS FOR YOU TO READ SO YOU DON'T KEEP BLOWING YOUR MIND ON THE GREAT SUBJECT.

LIKE IF YOU GOT QUESTIONS FOR EXAMPLE WHAT DOES A QUEER DO WHEN HE SEES A DOG. ANSWER IT DEPENDS ON THE DOG. MAYBE PETS IT.

ALSO DEPENDS ON WHOSE DOG. IF IT'S A NICE DOG WITH A MEAN MAN? ANSWER FEELS SORRY FOR THE DOG. IF IT'S A MEAN DOG WITH A NICE MAN. ANSWER FEELS SORRY FOR THE MAN. IF IT'S A NICE DOG WITH A NICE MAN. ANSWER MAKE FRIENDS!

HI

Hi Your dog is nice also you are

THANKS

Hi what's his name

LOOK OUT HE'S A QUEER

pooky do you think that's a dumb name

noway it's great

RUN FOR IT.

ALSO THERE'S PEOPLE WHO DON'T LIKE QUEERS. ONE THING THEY'RE THINKING IS THE QUEERS GOING TO KISS THEM

hey you! don't come near me

LIKE I WOULD EVER WANT TO

YOU DO SO WANT TO!

AS IF!

WHY NOT?

YOU GET ON MY NERVES

ANOTHER THING IS WHO IS A QUEER?
ANSWER MY UNCLE JOHN. ANOTHER
ONE IS BILL. THEY TOOK ME AND MY
SISTER TO THE DRIVE IN AND MY FRIEND
KEVIN TURNER. IT WAS SO GREAT BUT
NOW THAT THEY ARE KNOWN QUEERS
YOU CAN FORGET THAT WILL HAPPEN AGAIN
UNTIL THE MIRACLE DAY OF PEOPLE QUIT
BEING SO STUPID. WILL IT COME? I DON'T
KNOW.

I AM DOOMED

can Kevin come to the movies

not if queers will be there

There's usually queers at movies though.

Then forget it   ok BYE KEVIN

Sorry your moms BERSURK.

THERE'S PEOPLE WHO
WILL HIT YOU IF
THEY FIND OUT
YOU ARE QUEER.

MY UNCLE JOHN
HAS A SCAR ON HIS
FOREHEAD FROM IT.
THE POLICE SAID
"FORGET IT."

PERSONALLY I LIKE QUEERS!!! SO FAR
I ONLY KNOW TWO QUEERS AND I AM
LOOKING FOR MORE QUEERS!!! SO IF
YOU SEE ME PLEASE SAY HI DON'T BE
ALL SNOBBISH!!! ALSO IF YOU KNOW
OTHER QUEERS TELL THEM "MARLYS
SAYS HI." SAY "RIGHT ON FROM MARLYS"
AND DO THE POWER SIGN. AND IF YOU
SEE MY UNCLE JOHN AND BILL PLEASE
SAY I MISS THEM AND COME BACK SOON.

Love truely,
* Marlys *
P.S. heres my school
picture if you want
to stick it in your
billfold!!! It would
be an honor!!!

MARLYS GIFT SHOP

BY LYNDA BARRY and Julie Wilson! ©1991

SAY IF YOU HAVE TO GIVE SOMEONE A PRESENT! A GREAT PRESENT! WELL HERES SOME IDEAS FROM THE GREAT MARLYS!

FAKE EYE LASHES!

FREE onion rings!

ALL KINDS OF BEADED FRUIT + VEGETABLES!

TNT

BEAUTIFUL BICYCLE DECOR!

A PORTABLE RECORD PLAYER

LUDEN'S CHERRY COUGH DROPS

PIG iron!

Funner glasses!

A CROWN!

Perfume from paree!

a spider on a stick!

PERMISSION TO ROCK OUT! NAME.......

A MEXICAN HAT!

WHITE GO-GO BOOTS!

WATER SKIIS

glasses with a nose + moustache!

Incredible cake with Gorgeous Decorations!

VENUS FLY TRAP! (WATCH OUT, THOUGH)

TRES-SY

OUR DOMESTIC POULTRY

BY LYNDA "TAKE A LETTER MARIA" BARRY ☺ © 1991

Workbook p. 36 chap. 6
Marlys Mullen

Our Domestic Poultry
by Marlys Mullen

Chickens are old. In china there was chickens 3,000 years ago. In India. In the Indies. In Columbus. He ate them. They came to the USA on boats.

here Col. Sanders! a present

Pilgrim

What is it?

The name OF It is a chicken

Oh thank you now I got a job!

I will call it finger licking good!

Theres 2 kinds of chickens. Useful and Fancy Fancy ones are just for looks. To run in your yard to make it look beautiful.

Come Back!

NO ONE RUNS FROM COL. Sanders.

Fancy   USEFUL

The useful ones make eggs and also you eat them. Theres lots of varieties. But they all hate Col. Sanders. (Thats a joke, son!) People have fixed it so useful chickens cannot fly. That can be called cold blooded. They have 3 stomachs. They eat chicken—feed but they will eat Fritos.

2. proventriculus

1. crop

3. gizzard

Food in a chicken will not Get chewed! So Don't give them Gum not even Dentene. It goes down to the first stomach called Crop. Then into proventriculus. then Gizzard where theres rocks (actual) grinding it. The rest is usual.

A certain chicken can lay 300 Eggs a year! It is done by breeding.

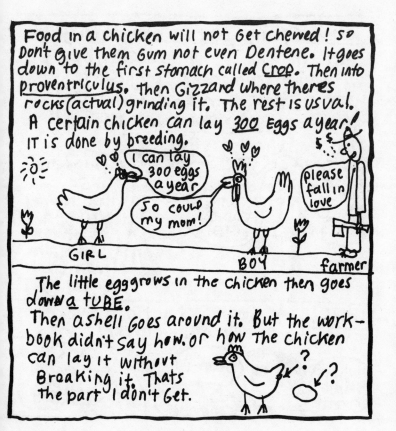

I can lay 300 eggs a year

So could my mom!

please fall in love

GIRL

BOY

farmer

The little egg grows in the chicken then goes down a TUBE.

Then a shell Goes around it. But the workbook didn't say how. or how The chicken can lay it without Breaking it. Thats the part I don't Get.

IT TAKES ABOUT 21 DAYS For The Chick TO Grow In the EGG then They Poke a hole In the Shell With the BEAK. Some chicks WILL Grow up TO LAY EGGS. OTHER CHICKS WILL grow Up TO BE Meat or Fried Chicken. Except very smart Fast runners.

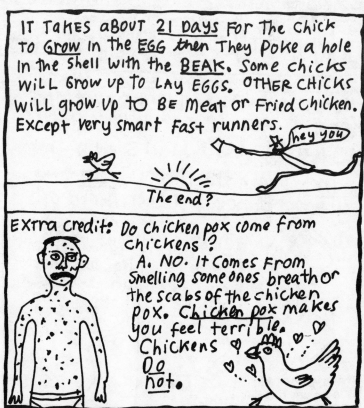

hey you

The end?

Extra credit: Do chicken pox come from chickens?

A. NO. It Comes From Smelling some ones breath or the scabs of the chicken pox. Chicken pox makes you feel terrible. Chickens Do not.

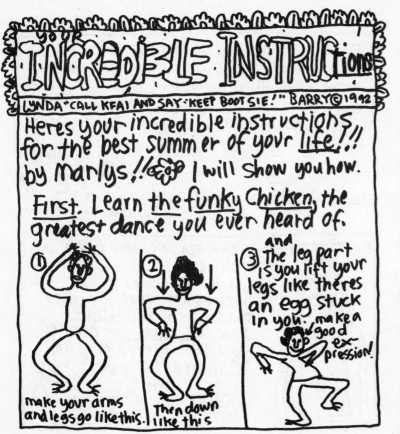

FORTH Enter a talent contest at the parking lot of the Dags Drive-in.

and the winner is

marlys!

For her Funky Chicken dancing that everyone says, right on to.

Thank you thank you please stop clapping!

TALent show

FIFTH Share your prize of 100 Hamburgers, French fries and orange drink with the RIGHT on people!

mmm Thanks marlys

ITS great!

marlys you are so great to give everyone this food and you smell incredible

yey marlys

OH please everyone it is nothing!

now you are popular, gorgeous, have great odors and can dance so of course you will have a perfect summer! by Marlys!!! your true friend and helper.!!. Right on!

marlys can you even help me?

Im sorry no MR president you will never be funky.

am I doing it?

vice pres ident

P.S. this Instructions is dedicated to my sister Maybonne who is depressed about the messed up world. from your number one secret Admirer!!!

YOU'RE SUPPOSED TO

BY LYNDA "SEE BARN" BARRY ✿ ✿ ✿ ✿ ©1991

DEAR BRENDA I AM WRITING YOU AGAIN EVEN THOUGH I HAVEN'T GOT A LETTER BACK FROM YOU YET DON'T WORRY ABOUT IT THOUGH, IT'S NO BIG. I AM <u>SO BORED</u>.!!!! ALSO I GOT 400 MOSQUITO BITES FROM SNEAKING OUTSIDE LAST NIGHT.

TAKE ME SWIMMING. TAKE ME DOWN TO CROFTON PARK.

NO.

I'LL BUST YOU FOR SNEAKING OUT LAST NIGHT.

NO YOU WON'T

CINDY LUDERMYER FROM NEXT DOOR RE-MEMBER I TOLD YOU ABOUT HER THE ONE WHO DOESN'T KNOW IF SHE'S A VIRGIN OR NOT-IF I DIDN'T TELL YOU LET ME KNOW AND I'LL WRITE IT IT'S AN INCREDIBLE STORY-SHE HAD A SNEAK OUT PARTY LAST NIGHT BY THIS THING WE CALL THE ROPE.

PLEASE?

NO.

PLEASE?

NO.

PLEASE?

NO.

PLEASE?

IT'S A ROPE HANGING IN THE WOODS BY THE RIVER YOU'RE SUPPOSED TO SWING ON IT OVER THE WATER AND LET GO. LAST NIGHT THEY WERE CALLING ME CHICKEN. FOR TWO THINGS. I WOULDN'T LET GO OF THE ROPE AND I WOULDN'T PLAY THIS STUPID GAME WHERE AROUND SIX GUYS FRENCH YOU. I LEFT EVEN THOUGH NO ONE ELSE WAS LEAVING LET THEM THINK I'M A PRUDE.

OK.

OK?

YEAH. LET'S GO.

YOU TRICKING ME?

THREE OF THE GUYS WERE OK BUT THREE OF THEM WERE SO FAKE. CINDY BARELY KNOWS THEM EVEN BUT THEY ARE GUYS AND TO HER GUYS COUNT MORE SO THAT'S WHY I'M BORED THEY ARE ALL AT CROFTON POOL TODAY AND FOR SOME REASON I DIDN'T FEEL LIKE GOING. YOU WERE NEVER LIKE THAT TO ME WITH GUYS BRENDA. I HOPE YOU WILL WRITE ME BACK SOON I'M MISSING YOU.

Love, Maybonne

THERE'S CINDY LUDERMYER.

WHO'S ALL THOSE GUYS?

CRO SWIL POO

57

MORE BOYS

BY LYNDA "I DO <u>NOT</u> FEEL GROOVY" BARRY © 1991

GUYS. CINDY LUDERMYER IS SO INTO GUYS AND GUYS ARE SO INTO CINDY LUDERMYER BUT NOT IN THE FOR REAL WAY. THEY ARE INTO HER IN THE GIANT BOOB WAY. THERE'S GIRLS I KNOW WHO HATE CINDY FOR THAT.

WHERE YOU GOIN'?

NO PLACE. GO BACK TO SLEEP.

BUT EVEN THEY'RE NOT HATING HER IN THE FOR REAL WAY. HARDLY ANYBODY FEELS FOR REAL ABOUT CINDY BECAUSE BEFORE YOU CAN GET TO THE FOR REAL PART, FIRST YOUR MIND HAS TO TRIP OUT ON HER INCREDIBLE BOD THAT JUST SORT OF GREW. IN A MOVIE PEOPLE WOULD LIKE CINDY BETTER IF SHE PRETENDED NOT TO NOTICE AND WORE NOT NOTICING OUTFITS.

IF YOU'RE SNEAKING OUT I'M COMING WITH YOU.

NO WAY.

I AM SO. WHY SHOULD YOU GET ALL THE FUN IN LIFE?

INSTEAD SHE WEARS THE TIGHTEST POOR-BOY SHIRTS WITH THE ZIPPER DOWN THE FRONT AND THE TIGHTEST HIP HUGGERS AND THE BLACKEST MABELLINE AND BOTH GIRLS AND BOYS HAVE SAID IT: SLUT, SLUT, SLUT. BUT NO ONE SAYS IT TO HER FACE. ALL SHE KNOWS IS RIGHT NOW THERES MORE BOYS AND LESS GIRLS IN HER LIFE AND A WINDOW SHE CAN SNEAK OUT OF AFTER HER PARENTS ARE ASLEEP.

FORGET IT. GO BACK TO SLEEP.

MARLYS.

OK. OK. OK.

AND TONIGHT SHE WANTS ME TO GO WITH HER. "I NEED YOU TO GUARD ME" SHE SAYS. IT'S THE NEW BOYS FROM THE CATHOLIC SCHOOL SHE'S MEETING TONIGHT AT CROFTON PARK, 1AM, BY THE ROPE. I SAY, "I'M NOT SURE." SHE SAYS, "PLEASE. COME ON. I'M BEGGING YOU."

59

IT'S COOL

BY LYNDA "BACHELOR PARTY" BARRY © 1991

"THERE'S JUST SOME THINGS THAT MEN HAVE TO KEEP TO THEMSELVES." IS WHAT THE BOY EDDIE DAVIS SAID WHEN I GOT TO THE SNEAK OUT PLACE WHERE I WAS SUPPOSED TO MEET CINDY LUDERMYER. IT WAS 1 AM AND SHE WASN'T THERE. ONLY EDDIE AND ANOTHER GUY VINCENT.

"SO SHE WAS ALREADY HERE THEN?" I ASK. EDDIE SAYS "MAYBE YES AND MAYBE NO." I GO, "QUIT BEING A SPAZ. WHERE IS SHE?" ON A ROCK I SEE HER SWEATER. THAT'S WHEN HE SAYS THE MEN THING AND WHEN VINCENT PUTS HIS ARM AROUND ME. "IT'S COOL." HE SAYS. "IT'S COOL. DON'T FREAK OUT." I GO "I'M NOT FREAKING OUT."

BUT I WAS FREAKING OUT. SLIGHTLY FREAKING OUT. FREAKING OUT FOR ME AND FREAKING OUT FOR CINDY WHO LOVES BOONES FARM APPLE WINE AND THERE'S THE BOTTLE EMPTY ON ITS SIDE BY THE ROCK. CINDY WHO I SAID I WOULD GUARD. "COME ON YOU GUYS TELL ME WHERE SHE'S AT." THEN A WALKING NOISE IN THE BUSHES. "CINDY?" I SAY. "CINDY?"

NO. IT'S DAN. THE ORIGINAL GUY OF THE CATHOLIC BOYS WHO CINDY LIKED. HE'S BRUSHING HIS PANTS OFF AND WIPING HIS MOUTH. "EDDIE." HE SAYS. "EDDIE." THEN HE POINTS INTO THE WOODS. "SHE'S ASKIN' FOR YOU." EDDIE GOES AND I TRY TO FOLLOW. "HEY." DAN SAYS. HE PUSHES HIS HANDS AGAINST MY SHOULDERS. "DON'T FREAK OUT, MAN. IT'S COOL. IT'S COOL."

61

SHE WANTED IT
SHE WANTED IT

MARLYS SAW IT. SHE SAW THOSE GUYS AND CINDY LUDERMYER. SHE HID IN THE BUSHES AND WATCHED CINDY PUSHING ON THE GUY AND THE GUY PUSHING ON CINDY. AND IT WAS MARLYS THAT THREW THE ROCK.

MARLYS.

WHAT?

YOU OK?

QUIT ASKIN' ME THAT.

"YOU LITTLE BITCH!" IS WHAT THE GUY CALLED MY SISTER. IT WAS HER FIRST TIME OF THAT NAME. HE CAUGHT HER AND DRAGGED HER AND SAID TO HIS FRIENDS "WHAT ARE WE GOING TO DO NOW?"

QUIT STARIN' AT ME.

CINDY WAS SO DRUNK. SHE WAS CRYING. LAYING IN THE LEAVES AND THE STICKS AND CRYING. I KICKED THE GUYS LEG WHO WAS HOLDING ME AND HE KNOCKED ME IN THE HEAD. TWO GUYS RAN. ONE GUY POINTED AT CINDY AND SAID "SHE STARTED IT." AND HELD HIS CIG PACK TO ME LIKE "DID I WANT ONE."

MARLYS...

I ALREADY TOLD YOU A HUNDRED TIMES!!

IT WAS THE GUY CINDY LIKED. HE BENT TO HELP HER UP. "SEE?" HE SAYS. "SHE'S OK. CINDY. CINDY. YOUR FRIENDS ARE HERE." HE POINTS TO MARLYS WHO IS STANDING BY ME NOT MOVING. "YOU TELL ANYBODY AND THE WHOLE WORLD WILL KNOW WHAT A SLUT CINDY IS. YOU WANT THAT?"

I'M NOT TELLIN' ALL RIGHT? YOU SATISFIED?

63

StoP TaLKING

© 1991

BY LYNDA "BAD JAZZ GETS READY TO BLOW YOUR MIND" BARRY

CINDY LUDERMYER MADE ME SWEAR ON A STACK OF BIBLES NOT TO TELL WHAT HAPPENED IN THE WOODS WITH HER AND THE CATHOLIC SCHOOL GUYS. SHE SAID "AND HOW ARE WE GOING TO SHUT UP MARLYS?" BUT MARLYS HAS SHUT UP ON HER OWN.

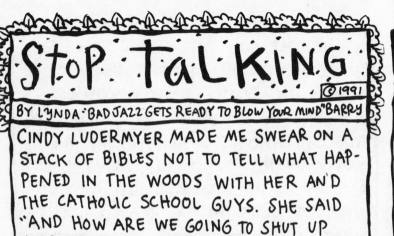

KUNG FU.

HAI KARATE!

SHE SAW THE GUYS AND SHE SAW CINDY BUT SHE HAS NEVER SAID ONE WORD EXCEPT HER NEW THING IS SHE WISHES SHE WAS A BOY. SHE TOLD ME THAT WAS THE NEXT WISH ON HER BIRTHDAY CAKE. I GO "HOW COME?" SHE GOES "EASIER LIFE." I TOLD CINDY DON'T WORRY ABOUT MARLYS.

UGH!

LIKE THE GUY ON TV!

CHOP CHOP CHOP CHOP CHOP

FOR THE LOVE OF GOD MARLYS! STOP IT!

WHO CINDY SHOULD BE WORRYING ABOUT IS HER OWN SELF. FOR AROUND ONE SECOND I SAID TO HER "TELL THE POLICE." AND SHE SAID "OH RIGHT." THEN SHE TOLD ME HOW HER PARENTS WOULD KILL HER. THEY WOULD TOO. EVEN THOUGH IT WASN'T HER FAULT. CINDY SAID WHO WOULD BELIEVE THAT?

YOU'VE HAD IT BUSTER!

CHOP!

CHOP CHOP!

MAYBONNE COME TALK TO YOUR SISTER BEFORE I WRING HER NECK!

ALSO, CATHOLIC BOYS VERSUS A PUBLIC GIRL. NO CONTEST ON WHO YOU WILL BELIEVE. OUR FATHER WHO ART IN HEAVEN, BUT YOU SAW, RIGHT? YOU SAW HER SAY NO AND THEM SAY YES. I TOLD HER "I THINK YOU SHOULD TELL." AND SHE TOLD ME "THAT'S EASY FOR YOU TO SAY." AND THEN SAID FOR ME TO JUST CHANGE THE SUBJECT.

MARLYS!

I KNOW! SHUT UP MARLYS! I KNOW! I KNOW!!

LOOKING DOWN

BY LYNDA "PLAY THAT ACCORDION!" BARRY © 1991

SOMEWHERE IN THE SKY FLOATING IN THE CLOUDS IS THE GIANT EYEBALL OF GOD LOOKING DOWN ON ME AND CINDY LUDER- MYER WALKING TO SCHOOL. CINDY IS NERVOUS. WORD GOT OUT ON HER AND THOSE GUYS IN THE WOODS.

IT'S COLD ENOUGH TO FINALLY WEAR A JACKET AND I AM SO THANKFUL. EVER SINCE THE NIGHT OF THOSE *BOYS* I HAVE BEEN WANTING TO PUT MORE AND MORE CLOTHES ON. CINDY HAS ON JUST A DRESS. SHE SAYS SHE'S NOT COLD BUT ANYONE CAN SEE THE GOOSEBUMPS ON HER ARMS.

SHE TELLS ME "WHO CARES WHAT EVERYONE THINKS." SHE OPENS HER PURSE AND TRIES TO HAND ME A CIG. "NO THANKS." I WATCH HER LIGHT IT AND PINCH HER EYES TOGETHER. THROUGH THE TREES AND TELEPHONE WIRES COMES THE SOUND OF THE FIRST BELL. "COME ON" I SAY. "LET'S SKIP FIRST PERIOD." SHE SAYS.

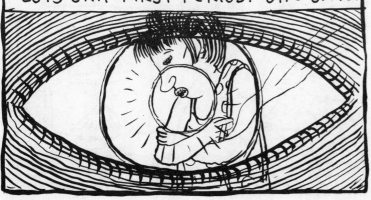

"CAN'T." I WANT TO BE IN A ROOM WHERE EVERYONE IS QUIET AND SITTING IN ROWS. THOSE BOYS GOT AWAY WITH IT. THEY GOT AWAY WITH IT. PEOPLE SAY IT WAS CINDY WHO CAUSED THE WHOLE THING. "COME ON." I SAY. SECOND BELL. CINDY JUST LOOKS AT ME. I SAY "COME ON." ONE MORE TIME, THEN TAKE OFF RUNNING.

67

IT'S NOTHING

by Lynda "SLEEP TIGHT" Barry © 1991

WE WERE LAYING IN CINDY'S BEDROOM. IT WASN'T ME WHO BROUGHT IT UP. "I GOT GEORGE." SHE SAYS. OUR CODE WORD FOR HOW SHE KNEW SHE WASN'T PREGNANT. "IF I WAS," SHE SAID, "I WOULD HAVE KILLED MYSELF."

I STILL WANT HER TO TELL THE POLICE ON THOSE GUYS. SHE SAYS IT'S ALL READY TOO LATE. NO ONE WOULD BELIEVE HER NOW. "BUT YOU GOT WITNESSES!" I SAY. "I SAW AND MARLYS SAW!" SHE SAID WHO WAS GOING TO BELIEVE ME AND MARLYS?

68

"THEY'LL SAY I STARTED **EVERYTHING** BECAUSE **OF** IT WAS ME THAT SCORED THE WINE AND SAID WHERE TO MEET." THEN SHE TELLS ME AGAIN HOW STUPID SHE IS. I TELL HER NO SHE ISN'T. I TELL HER THAT IF WE BUST THEM AT LEAST THEY MIGHT GET EXPELLED. SHE SAID PEOPLE WILL SAY SHE IS TRYING TO WRECK THEIR FUTURE.

"PLUS," SHE SAYS, "MY PARENTS WILL KILL ME IF THEY FIND OUT I'M NOT A VIRGIN." SHE ROLLS ONTO HER STOMACH AND PUTS HER FACE DOWN ON HER ARMS. "ANYWAY, IT'S NOTHING. I DON'T KNOW WHY I KEEP MAKING A BIG DEAL OUT OF IT. IT'S NOT LIKE IT REALLY EVEN BOTHERS ME THAT MUCH." THEN SHE'S QUIET AND WHEN I LOOK OVER, HER SHOULDERS ARE SHAKING.

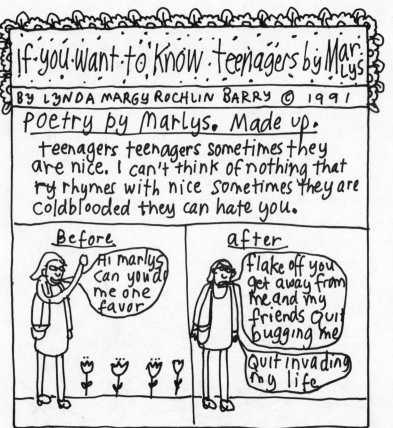

If you want to know teenagers by Marlys

BY LYNDA MARGY ROCHLIN BARRY © 1991

poetry by Marlys. Made up.

teenagers teenagers sometimes they are nice. I can't think of nothing that ry rhymes with nice sometimes they are coldblooded they can hate you.

Before

Hi marlys can you do me one favor

after

flake off you get away from me and my friends Quit bugging me

Quit invading my life

they can look beautiful. beautiful make up clothes handwriting.

I am so ugly

Do you think so

Front View. The front side

I messed up side view

sorry it is ugly!

they can get worried. people yelling at them when they already got bummer problems makes them ride on more bummers.

Why do you act like this Its your friend Cindy the rotten infwence on you. Now you can't see her!

She is my best friend

LIKE I CARE!

please no.

When they are riding on bummers you must watch out. Could be they want to talk to you. Could be they will yell in your face. But can you remember they are sad.

COULD BE

why does the whole world hate me

COULD BE

I hate you!!!!

If its your sister who yells one good thing is sometimes she is sorry after.

She don't look this spazzy in real life sorry on my crud drawing

sorry marlys

That is OK That is not even a prob!

me in the future →

One main thing you got to know is they have secrets. you must not bust them on the secrets. Teenagers teenagers theres things that they do. And if you tell anyone they will cream you.

Sorry for no picture.
I saw something I
can't even draw it.
Don't try to guess it.
Just forget it.

HOME SWEET HOME

by LYNDA "MAUSTON" BARRY ❦ © 1991 ❦

I GOT SOME NEWS. IT'S INCREDIBLE NEWS. DID YOU ALREADY KNOW I HAVE A BROTHER? FREDDY. ONE YEAR YOUNGER THAN MARLYS. WHEN MOM WENT THROUGH HER CHANGES ME AND MARLYS CAME HERE AND FREDDY WENT TO AUNT MAY, THE AUNT I DON'T LIKE WHO I'M SEMI-NAMED AFTER.

WELL LOOK HOW BIG YOU ARE!

HOW WAS THE AIRPLANE RIDE?

FINE.

WERE YOU SCARED?

NO.

SHE ALREADY HAS TWO KIDS, OUR COUSINS ARNA AND ARNOLD. NOW AUNT MAY IS GOING THROUGH HER CHANGES AND ONE OF THE THINGS SHE CHANGED IS HER MIND ABOUT KEEPING FREDDY. I'M NOT TALKING ABOUT CHANGE-OF-LIFE CHANGES. I MEAN A FREAK-OUT LIKE THE FREAK-OUT OF MY MOM. I THINK IT'S RUNNING IN THE FAMILY. THIS MORNING GRANDMA TOLD US "FREDDY'S COMING."

THIS IS MR. LUDERMYER

HI.

HEY THERE CHAMP! YOUR GRANDMA'S TOLD ME ALL ABOUT YOU!

FOR A LONG TIME I COULDN'T EVEN SAY THE NAME OF FREDDY BECAUSE THEN <u>MAR-LYS</u> WOULD HAVE A FREAK-OUT. FOR AROUND THREE MONTHS OF US BEING HERE SHE ASKED FOR FREDDY. THEN SHE QUIT. HIS ROOM IS GOING TO BE IN THE BASEMENT. ME AND MARLYS SPENT ALL DAY FIXING IT UP. MARLYS BEGGED OFF A LOAD OF ALFRED E. NEWMANS FROM HER FRIEND KEVIN TURNER. SHE REMEMBERED FREDDY LOVES THOSE.

YOU OK IN THE BACK SEAT?

YEAH.

YOU EXCITED ABOUT SEEING YOUR SISTERS?

AND WE GOT THE HOUSE ALL CLEAN AND MARLYS MADE HER LONG SIGN ON A ROW OF PAPER TOWELS "WELCOME HOME FREDDY." I TOLD HER THIS ISN'T EXACTLY HOME SO MAYBE SHE SHOULD LEAVE THAT WORD OFF BUT SHE SAID IF THE HOUSE HAD <u>ME</u> IN IT, AND <u>HER</u> IN IT, <u>AND</u> FREDDY IN IT, THEN THE JUDGES SAY THAT EQUALS HOME. I TRIED ASKING HER "WHAT JUDGES?" BUT THE FRONT DOOR OPENED. IT OPENED AT LAST.

WELL, HERE HE IS, EVERYBODY!

QUIT TALKING

BY LYNDA "IT'S ISOTONER!" BARRY ❀ © 1991

MY BROTHER FREDDY HAD HIS FIRST DAY AT HIS NEW SCHOOL. MARLYS SHOWED HIM EVERYTHING: WHERE HIS ROOM WAS, THE OFFICE, THE LUNCHROOM AND WHICH STEPS YOU CAN'T STEP ON BECAUSE THEY'RE CONTAMMINATED.

HE MET HIS NEW TEACHER MRS. HORTY WHO SAID "OH LORD" WHEN SHE FOUND OUT HE WAS THE BROTHER OF MARLYS. THE BOOKMOBILE CAME AND FREDDY GOT A LIBRARY CARD. HE CHECKED OUT A BOOK ON BATS CALLED <u>BATS BATS BATS</u> WHICH HE HAS TO DO A BOOK REPORT ON. A GIRL NAMED CINDY KICKED HIM IN THE LEG AT LUNCH.

IN HIS SPELLING BOOK THERE WERE ALREADY A LOT OF DRAWINGS ON THE PICTURES. FREDDY SAID THE GUY WHO HAD THE BOOK BEFORE HIM COULD DRAW VERY REALISTIC HAND GRENADES, BOSOMS, FRANKENSTEIN NECK BOLTS AND LIT BOMBS. DURING P.E. HE GOT HIT IN THE FACE WITH A WET BALL. ON ACCIDENT.

DURING MUSIC HE CHOSE FINGER CYMBALS OUT OF THE BOX AND GOT CALLED A QUEER. IN SCIENCE HE KNEW THAT MAMMELS HAD HAIR BEFORE THE TEACHER SAID IT. IN MATH HE DID GOOD ON THE PROBLEMS. HE MET A GUY NAMED RICHIE WHO MIGHT BE HIS FRIEND AND HE WOULD HAVE TOLD US MORE BUT GRANDMA SAID "QUIT TALKING WITH YOUR MOUTH FULL." AND HIS FEELINGS GOT HURT FOR THE REST OF THE NIGHT.

HE'S JUST LIKE HIS FATHER.

PICTURE CONTEST

BY LYNDA. DA BROS. " BARRY ☺ VIVA WISCONSIN! © 1991

I COME DOWNSTAIRS AND AT THE TABLE THERE'S MARLYS AND FREDDY MAKING THANKSGIVING TURKEY DRAWINGS FOR THE GROCERY STORE PICTURE CONTEST. "WE'RE GOING TO WIN." SAYS MARLYS. I'M STILL NOT USED TO SEEING MY LITTLE BROTHER IN THIS HOUSE.

HE HOLDS UP HIS PAPER. IT'S NOT JUST BECAUSE HE'S MY BROTHER THAT I SAY IT IS GORGEOUS. "FIVE MORE MINUTES" MARLYS TELLS ME, "AND YOU'RE WALKING US DOWN TO THE STORE." IN MY BROTHER'S FACE I SEE DAD. I SEE MOM. I SEE MARLYS. I SEE ME. "PUT A CROWN ON YOUR TURKEY" SAYS MARLYS. "THE KING AND QUEEN OF TURKEYS!"

AT THE STORE THE LADY HANDS US SCOTCH TAPE AND POINTS TO THE LOADED UP WINDOW. "ANYWHERE YOU WANT," SHE SAYS. I HELP MARLYS AND FREDDY TAPE THEIRS UP AND WATCH THEM RUN OUTSIDE TO LOOK THROUGH THE GLASS. MARLYS AND FREDDY CRACKING UP LAUGHING. WHAT WAS SO FUNNY WAS THE MIDGET TURKEY DINGER FREDDY DREW ON. IT BLENDED IN BUT YOU COULD ALSO NOTICE IT.

THE WINNER AND CHAMPION GOT ANNOUNCED AT 4:30. THAT'S THE REASON YOU SAW IT: TWO KIDS HAULING A HEAVY TURKEY DOWN CONGRESS STREET. THEIR PRIZE. AND THEY WOULD NOT LET ANYONE HELP THEM. IT WAS FREDDY'S IDEA TO MAKE A CARRYING HAMMOCK WITH HIS SKI-JACKET. THEY DROPPED IT ABOUT FOUR TIMES ON THE WAY TO GRANDMAS BUT IT DID NOT AFFECT THE TASTE OR OUR GREAT THANKSGIVING DAY.

SOME EMPLOYMENT.

BY LYNDA "CALMING EYEBALL" BARRY ©1991

MY BROTHER FREDDY AND MY SISTER MARLYS HAVE DECIDED WHAT THEY WANT FOR THEIR JOBS OF THE FUTURE: STUNTMAN AND STUNT WOMAN. FREDDY SAYS HE WILL JUMP FROM HUNDRED FOOT TOWERS. MARLYS SAYS SHE WILL TANGLE WITH WILD BOARS AND MAN EATING SHARKS. THEY SAY THEY WILL BOTH MAKE HAIR-RAISING ESCAPES.

THE INCREDIBLY INCREDIBLE STUNTMAN and Lady Book of all time!

LOOKOUT! IT'S A BOMB!
yes I know!
and I am holding it

FREDDY IS WRITING AN INSTRUCTION BOOK ON HOW TO BE A STUNTMAN AND MARLYS IS DRAWING THE PICTURES.

page 1 Once upon a time was the most incredible job you could ever have! Main example? You got the job of Stunt man! or Stunt lady! or if you want call it stunt woman! What did you get to do?

1. a ganster threw you down stairs!
why you dirty rat you killed my brother
AHAHA

2. you got shot off a roof By the Marshall!
This town ain't big enough for both of us.
BLAM BLAM
AAhhhh
← fake bullet holes

HE SAYS IT WILL HAVE 679 THRILLING PAGES AND 900 ACTION DRAWINGS.

Page 2) In the lair of evil you meet the Killer snake!

4. Your bodys covered with Killer ants!

5. Get smashed on the head by a bottle in a bar!

TAKE That
Konk!

6. Get the kiss of death from some lady in a long dress and long finger nails. no wait. maybe the stunt man doesn't do this. But maybe he does!

SO FAR HE ONLY HAS FOUR THRILLING PAGES AND 8 ACTION DRAWINGS BUT HE SAYS IT'S GOING TO BE NO PROBLEM.

For certain you will be also swinging from things a lot too! like: chandaliers! vines! trees! wires between houses! other stunt men!

your number one question is: am I cut out to be a stunt man or lady stuntwoman? Here's the test! Good luck may you get them right.

1. Do you care if people hurl you to your death a lot?

2. Is it ok with you if a wild dog bites on your jugular vein?

3. Would you jump in boiling lava?

4. Will you let 5 cars run over you?

5. Would you kiss on the lips with death?

ANSWER: 1. No! 2. sure! 3. Any day! 4. yes! 5. Probably!

Cooking With Freddy

BY LYNDA "PASS the COOKIES" BARRY © 1991

Say your sisters are hungry and you want to fix them a dinner here's a thing: <u>fried baloney sandwich!</u>
bread = carbohydrate, put on some lettuce = vegetable, the meat is the baloney. Drink it down with milk. Add it together it equals <u>FOUR</u> food groups!

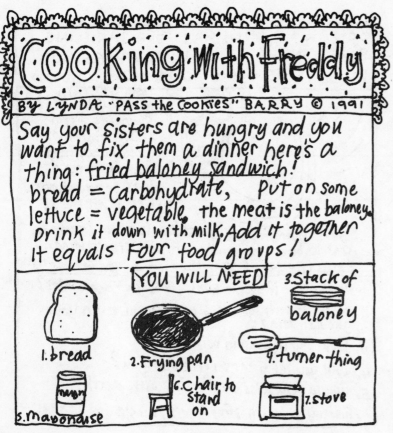

YOU WILL NEED

1. bread
2. Frying pan
3. Stack of baloney
4. turner thing
5. Mayonaise
6. chair to stand on
7. stove

① drag your chair to the stove and stick on the frying pan. Light up the stove. Peel open the baloney package. Peel off a baloney. Drop it onto the frying pan. If your sister tells you it's a waste of time because she's not going to like it she is <u>wrong</u>.

I WILL not like it

you are wrong

2] Keep your eyes on the baloney and wait for the magic. You **will** see it! The baloney will go in a hump. It will pop-up in the pan in slow motion. then turn it over and see the re-run. Fried baloney is very good a little burnt. Burnt on the edges is great. Then put mayonaise on the bread + the baloney + lettuce And the smell will be alluring.

she is floating on the oder

Come and get it!

mmmmm

I was spazzing out when I said I did not want some.

3] What is really good is if you also have potato chips to put in the sand-wich **and** a banana to eat with it. and a giant milk and what is _really_ good is if you eat it on TV trays in front of your favorite show. Try it on your sisters or anybody who is hungry and sad. It is the best food for sad people! That's all folks until next time from your world famous chef of cooking, the great Freddy!!

Freddy you are incredible and this sandwich is also very incredible!

the end

SORRY STORY

BY LYNDA "LOVE TO THE CAST AT THE REP!!!" BARRY © 1992

the worlds lonliest outpost of the atlantic adventure report by Freddie Mullen

In the middle of the atlantic ~~island~~ ocean is a little island made of rocks where only 200 people live. Theres more people at our school than the whole island called TristanDaCunha. Its an ugly island.

"Get me out of here I want to go to California"

"Quit bringing that up will you we are stuck here man"

One great thing about it is a 8,000 foot high volcano

"even our volcano is cruddy. I hate it here."

One bad thing is the volcano is ice cold

It got its name from the man who discovered it. A explorer. The people told him it already had a name. He told them "BIG DEAL"

First came people from Portugal then Scotland. They brought animals for the natives.

① "I will trade you this weiner dog for all your land" "Do you think I'm Burzurk?"

② "you should have taken the weiner dog" TILT

Then they showed the people their gods were fake outs.

① "But we love our gods." "If they're so great how come you never get anything for Chirstmas?"

② AAAA "Should have listened to me man." "at least now you can go to heaven."

Then the people came over from Holland, Italy, America and a lot of ships crashed and sank when they got there

"help! help"

"see! our gods aren't either fake outs!"

82

Then the brother of the guy that wrote ~~Ala~~ Alice in Wonderland came. He was a missionary. He Brought A Lot of his friends AND they got their WAY.

①

After awhile people from other lands got sick of this lonely Island And went back home. They didn't invite their new buddys who they taught to eat potatoes.

Now everyone lives in a little town around a BIG church. Now everyone is SICK OF potatoes. Now everyone is hoping a ship will come that they can sneak on And go to california. Until then the 200 people JUST FEEL sad And lonely.

In my opinion there are some people who ~~Should~~ SHOULD go Back to the place Called Tristan DaCUNha And Say they are sorry. IF I could go there I know I WOULD say it.

ARTISTIC PROJECTS

BY LYNDA "EATING BANANAS IN HOUSTON" BARRY © 1992

have you ever thought of this one? You can carve <u>gorgeous</u> in SOAP!! by The Great Marlys!!! ✱ ✱ ✱
<u>ALSO</u> and some ideas by the great Freddie!!

WHAT YOU NEED

SOAP
- IVORY
- SAFEGUARD
- DON'T YOU WISH YOU USE DIAL
- CAMAY
- DOVE ONE Quarter cleansing cream • DON'T TRY DISHWASHING LiQUID

KNIFE
Sharp is GOOD but your mom WiLL Say NO. So WAIT UNTIL She iS at work OR USE

<u>BUTTER KNiFE</u>

YOUR GREAT BRAINS
OF iMAGINATION!

OR ASK Freddie iF YOU ARE STUCK.

DIRECTIONS:

① Get YOUR SOAP. HARD SOAP IS the best DON'T TRY the SOAP THAT WAS LAYING IN THE TUB WITH YOU.

EXCUSE ME CAN I HAVE the SOAP?

I am Shy if you DON'T NOTICE!

hey you Get OUT DO you THINK this is A NUDIST COLONEY.

<u>Hints on SOAP:</u> ASK your mom first UNLESS She has A TON She got on SALE AND then forgot it Then just Sneak <u>ONE ONLY.</u> See iF You Can USE COLORS!!!

CAMAY = PINK! DIAL: ORANGE! iRish psychadelic SPRING: Green!

② <u>FIND A GOOD PLACE TO CARVE</u>

IN THE KITCHEN iF your mom already Knows.

UNDER the porch if She doesn't

84

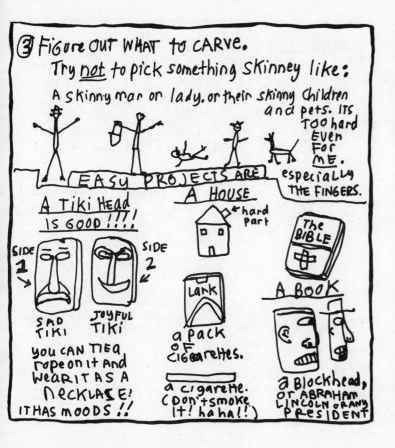

③ FIGURE OUT WHAT to CARVE.
Try __not__ to pick something SKINNEY like:

A skinny man or lady. or their skinny children and pets. ITS TOO hard EVEN FOR ME. especially THE FINGERS.

EASY PROJECTS ARE

A HOUSE
← hard part

A Tiki Head
IS GOOD !!!!

SIDE 1 →   ← SIDE 2

SAD TIKI   JOYFUL TIKI

you CAN TIE a rope on it and WEAR IT AS A NECKLACE! IT HAS MOODS !!

Lark
a PACK OF CIGarettes.

a cigarette. (Don't smoke It! ha ha !!)

The BIBLE

A BOOK

a Blockhead, or ABRAHAM LINCOLN or ANY PRESIDENT

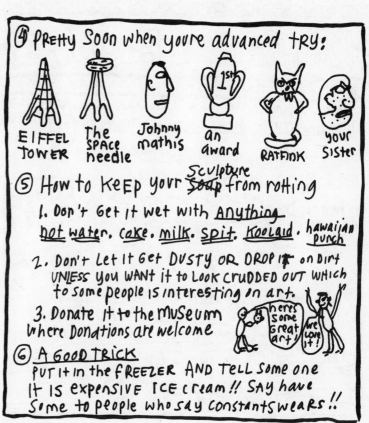

④ PRETTY SOON when you're advanced TRY:

EIFFEL TOWER   The SPACE needle   Johnny mathis   an award   RATFINK   your Sister

⑤ How to KEEP your ~~Soap~~ Sculpture from rotting

1. Don't Get it wet with __Anything__ __hot water__. __cake__. __milk__. __spit__. __Koolaid__. __hawaiian punch__

2. Don't Let it Get DUSTY OR DROP It on DIRT UNLESS you WANT it to Look CRUDDED OUT WHICH to some people Is interesting on art.

3. Donate it to the MUSEUM Where Donations are welcome

here's some Great art   we love it!

⑥ A GOOD TRICK
PUT It In the FREEZER AND TELL Some one It IS expensive ICE cream !! SAY have Some to people who say constant swears !!

85

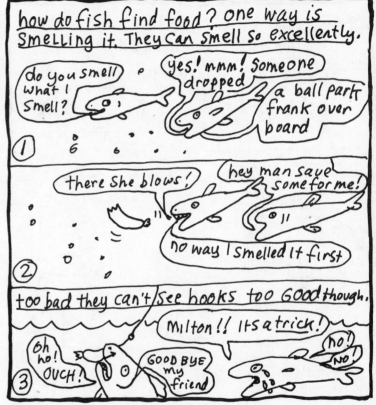

Some fish just eat the microscope things you see floating in most water. They open their mouths and hope things go in. The microscope things gets caught in them and turns to food. That's like you running in a parking lot with your mouth open until bugs fly in. These kinds of fish are more skinny than the kind who suddenly eat their friends without warning.

alphoso why are you staring at me like that?

alphonso does 20 days of friendship mean nothing to you?

Alphonso! I trusted you alphonso

AAAAHH!!

Some fish love bugs. They love to look up and see little bug feet wiggle on the water. It gets them so excited.

alphonso you crud I saw the way you ate David

oh a lushious bug!

Oh shut up

OR I'll eat you too.

And thats why you make your bait look like a bug. Good luck in your life from now on now that you got my advice sincerely yours Freddie

GOT one!

Pull him in!

ba ha ha serves you right alphonso

help!

Oh no! I fell for it!

BATS OF INTEREST

BY LYNDA "Winter Carnival in St. Paul!" BARRY © 1992

Freddie Mullen
extra credit re-
port. (Book)

Title: Bats Bats Bats
Author Timothy Latta Pages 64
How did you hear about the book my brother.

Bats Bats Bats

Bats Bats Bats is a incredible book. It is mostly about Bats who are our only mammals with wings. Where did Bats come from? Even scientists don't KNOW!

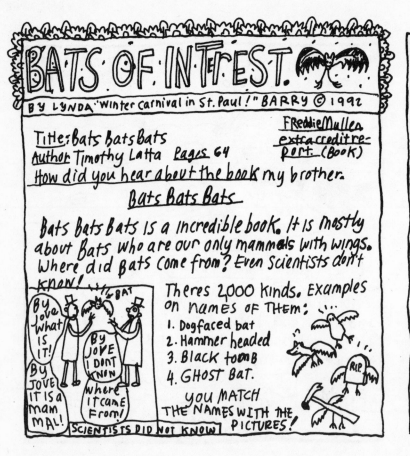

By Jove what IS it!

BAT

By Jove I don't know where it came from!

By Jove it is a mam MAL!

SCIENTISTS DID NOT KNOW

Theres 2000 kinds. Examples on names of them:
1. Dogfaced bat
2. Hammer headed
3. Black toomb
4. GHOST BAT.

YOU MATCH THE NAMES WITH THE PICTURES!

R.I.P.

Facts on Bats: They Fly with their mouths open And their noise bounces on things so they never crash. They believe in free love. The babies ride around on the moms, and the moms love them. If you STEAL a Baby Bat the Mom will try to LOCATE you. They can Live to be 20 years OLD.

← Baby

← mother

One kind called Noctilio or Bulldog Bat smells horrible. The Author says it is a Bad Odor. ~~~~~ said he picked up a Bulldog Bat and the smell stayed on his hands for around a WEEK even though he washed his hands

may I have this dance

Did you hold that same bat again?

I will dance with you next week

Vampire Bats are real. They have special stomach for digesting blood. First seen by Charles Darwin who also invented our thing with the monkeys. They're only around as long as your long finger and they can run on walls. They slit the veins of victims with sharp front teeth but they are so good at it you can't hardly feel it. Then they lick the blood. Not really a big deal except they have major germs on their tongues!

oh no!

what is it my dear

a bat is sucking your forehead!

and yet I feel nothing!

Oh honey theres one on you too

Bat Guano comes out of bats and people buy it. In the Civil war part of it made gunpowder and soldiers guarded it with guns.

hey buster I will blow your head OFF!

get away from it!

←Bat

↓guano

robber

soon the guano will be mine!

The Saddest Bats.
In world war two the U.S.A. tied bombs on free TAILED bats. Time Bombs that were even bigger then the bat! When it blew up the flame went 22 inches and burned for eight minutes. The plan was to blow up Japan and other enemies with bats that would fly the bombs into houses and buildings but then scientists finished the A-Bomb. Lucky for the bats. Unlucky for everyone else. I enjoyed Bats Bats Bats it is a great book for under-standing Bats! by Freddie!

the end?

Tick Tick Tick

89

A LONG TIME AGO

BY L Y N D A "WADING IN THE GULF" BARRY © 1991

REMEMBER A LONG TIME AGO I TOLD YOU ABOUT CINDY LUDERMYER'S BOYFRIEND AGNER WHO DROPPED OUT AND JOINED THE ARMY? WELL GUESS WHAT? SHE JUST GOT A LETTER FROM HIM. HE'S ALREADY AT THE WAR.

HE SAYS SO FAR THE WAR IS MOSTLY BORING AND IT'S HOT AND THERES A GUY IN HIS BUNKER WHO WON'T QUIT SPRAYING BUG SPRAY. HE SAYS THE EQUIPMENT HE HAS TO CARRY WEIGHS 65 POUNDS AND THAT A GUY DROWNED FROM HIS COMPANY BECAUSE HE WALKED IN THE WATER AND THE EQUIPMENT WAS TOO HEAVY FOR HIM TO GET BACK OUT.

AGNER SAYS NOT TO WORRY ABOUT HIM THOUGH AND THAT THE GUY WHO DROWNED WAS A JACKASS BUT HE DIDN'T EXPLAIN WHY HE WAS A JACKASS. AGNER IS IN COMPANY A, 4TH BATTALION, 59TH INFANTRY, 10TH INFANTRY DIVISION. WHATEVER THAT MEANS. I'M AGAINST WAR. AGNER SAYS HE THINKS OF CINDY ALL THE TIME.

HE SAYS THEY WERE GOING OUT THAT NIGHT TO A NEW PLACE WHERE VERY FOR REAL STUFF WOULD BE HAPPENING AND THAT HE HOPES CINDY IS BEING TRUE WHICH SHE ISN'T. SHE SHOWED ME THE LETTER. "WHAT SHOULD I DO?" SHE SAID. SHE WANTS TO KNOW SHOULD SHE TELL HIM ABOUT BILL IN A LETTER? OR JUST WAIT UNTIL AGNER GETS HOME.

A LOAD OF BALONEY

BY LYNDA · tools in the toolbox " BARRY ✲ ☺ © 1991

I WAS TALKING TO MR. LUDERMYER ABOUT THE WAR. I GUESS I'M FINALLY GETTING THAT WE'RE HAVING ONE. OUTSIDE THE WINDOW BEHIND HIS HEAD I COULD SEE THE MOON JUST SHINING SHINING SHINING.

HE SAYS WE'RE INTO SOMETHING WE CAN'T GET OUT OF SO ALL MY PEACE CRAP IS A LOAD OF BALONEY AND HE SAID WHAT ARE WE WAITING FOR WE SHOULD JUST BOMB THE HELL OUT OF THEM AND I SAID I THOUGHT WE ALREADY WERE AND HE SAID HE DOESN'T MEAN THE PISS-ANT BOMBS WE'RE USING.

RIGHT WHEN HE SAYS THAT I SEE THE LIGHTS OF A PLANE AND I TRY TO IMAGINE IF IT HAD BOMBS, PISS-ANT OR REGULAR, AND ON THE RADIO WOULD COME THE SOUND OF THIS IS A TEST OF THE EMERGENCY BROADCAST SYSTEM EXCEPT THIS TIME IT'S NOT ONLY A TEST. I HAVE SEEN MOVIES OF BOMBS COMING DOWN. FIRST YOU HEAR THE SIREN AND THEN YOU START RUNNING.

THEN <u>BLAM</u>! A BOOKSHELF FALLS OVER IN THE FRONT ROOM. MRS. LUDERMYER WAS TRYING TO VACCUM BEHIND IT. "JESUSCHRISTSONOFABITCH!" SHOUTS MR. LUDERMYER. THE ENCYCLOPEDIA ALL OVER THE FLOOR AND SMASHED CUPS FROM ENGLAND. THE FISH FROM THE FISH BOWL TWISTING IN OXYGEN. I HOLD THEM IN MY HANDS AND RUN TO WHERE THERE'S WATER. OUR FATHER WHO ART IN HEAVEN I DON'T EVEN KNOW WHAT TO SAY TO YOU ANYMORE.

THE PRESIDENT KNOWS

BY LYNDA "HUNKER IN THE BUNKER" BARRY © 1991

CINDY GOT ANOTHER LETTER FROM AGNER. HE TOLD HER HE CAN'T SAY WHERE HE IS BECAUSE OF SECURITY BUT THEY ARE GOING ON A HARD SORTIE AND THEY JUST CAME FROM A HARD SORTIE. NEITHER ME OR CINDY KNOW FOR SURE WHAT'S A SORTIE.

WHO'S YOUR LETTER TO?

MIKE

HE SAID ONE BUDDY DIED BECAUSE HE BENT DOWN TO PICK UP HIS LIGHTER AND AGNER SAYS HE'S NOT REALLY SURE WHY THERES A WAR BUT THE PRESIDENT KNOWS SO AGNERS MAIN THING IS JUST DO HIS JOB AND REMEMBER WHEN THERES MOTARS KEEP YOUR HEAD DOWN.

WHO'S MIKE?

GUY IN THE WAR.

94

ALSO WATCH CHANNEL SEVEN BE-CAUSE THE TV WAS THERE AND AGNER MIGHT BE ON. IT'S THE ONE WHERE THEY TAKE A GUY IN A HELOCOPTER WITH HIS LEG BLOWN OFF. WE HAVE SEEN A LOT OF GUYS WITH PARTS BLOWN OFF BUT WE HAVEN'T SEEN AGNER.

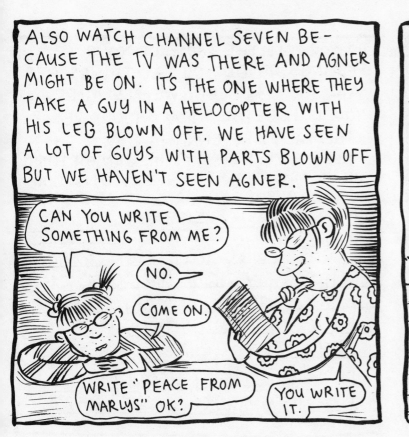

CAN YOU WRITE SOMETHING FROM ME?

NO.

COME ON.

WRITE "PEACE FROM MARLYS" OK?

YOU WRITE IT.

HE SAYS HE JUST HAS TWO DREAMS AT NIGHT. NUMBER ONE HE'S BACK HOME AND NUMBER TWO PEOPLE ARE TRYING TO KILL HIM. THE SOUND OF BOMBS AND SHOOTING STAYS IN YOUR HEAD A LONG TIME ACCORDING TO AGNER AND HE ALWAYS LOOKS AT CINDY'S PICTURE. HIS P.S. WAS HE HAS A BUDDY WHO WANTS CINDYS FRIENDS TO WRITE HIM. HIS NAME IS MIKE. "OK" I TOLD CINDY.   I WILL DO IT.

P.S. Dear Mike right on what is happening! how are you this is marlys her sister Can I just say something to you peace!!! and I hope you dont die! or no one else does! and write me back. My own letter!! I will always remember you and always write you back! ⊘ ☮ ← peace sign by Marlys

Dear Mike,

by LYNDA "FRIENDLY FIRE" BARRY 🌸🌸🌸🌸🌸 © 1991

WHAT DO YOU WRITE IN A LETTER TO A SOLDIER? PLEASE DON'T GET KILLED? PLEASE DON'T KILL SOMEONE ELSE? OR: DORITOS GOTS A NEW FLAVOR.

○ Dear Mike remember It's Marlys what is happening. Maybonne says for me not to draw no peace signs because It can hurt your feelings. Is
○ this
☐ true   ☐ False

DO YOU TELL THE TRUTH OF YOUR FEELINGS OR DO YOU SAY "THINGS ARE ALL RIGHT EXCEPT WE ALL MISS YOU." IS IT DETAILS YOU SHOULD TELL? LIKE "THEY ARE CLOSING DOWN THE FROSTEE FREEZE BY THE JUNIOR HIGH" OR IS IT OK TO ASK QUESTIONS LIKE "WHEN A PERSON DROPS A BOMB DOES HE EVER FEEL BAD?"

I say false because I do not think you dig on war. automatically don't you want peace? My sister says thats sticking my nose in your business if you dont like peace signs how about flowers I draw them Good

THE PRESIDENT SAYS WE MUST FIGHT OVER THERE BECAUSE <u>WE</u> <u>ARE</u> <u>AMERICANS</u> WHICH SEEMS SO FAKEY TO ME. IF HE IS GOING TO MAKE PEOPLE BOMB AND GET BOMBED HE COULD AT LEAST BE FOR REAL ABOUT THE REASON. EVEN A STUPID REASON'S BETTER THAN A FAKE OUT.

I see soldiers on the TV every night If you get on wave hi Marlys too me OK Mike. What can I send you as a present Do you have a viewmaster I got extra cards. Well that is all I know to say except no offence. peace.

THE GUY I'M WRITING TO, MIKE, WANTS TO KNOW WHAT EVERYBODY IS THINKING ABOUT THE WAR. WHICH PEOPLE SHOULD I TELL HIM ABOUT? MR. LUDERMYER WHO SAYS DROP THE A-BOMB? OR THE ONES WHO THINK I'M A TRAITOR TO PEACE FOR EVER EVEN WRITING MIKE? OR SHOULD I JUST DO LIKE OUR PRESIDENT AND SAY THE FAKE OUT WORDS OF: EVERYTHING IS GREAT, MIKE. EVERYTHING IS GOING JUST GREAT.

I wish you come Back soon mike! ~~Nou~~ If you could come back we could all have a very nice time truthfully. dont you want it. your truely Marlys

97
T.N.T.

HOW BAD

by LYNDA "THE FOG OF WAR" BARRY © 1991

CINDY GOT ANOTHER LETTER FROM AGNER WHO SAID THINGS ARE VERY HAIRY AND GETTING MORE HAIRY. HE SAID THE DINKS FIGHT A LOT BETTER THAN HE THOUGHT. DINKS IS ONE OF THE WORDS FOR ENEMY.

PEACE, MAN.

SAY IT BACK.

C'MON MAYBONNE

HIS QUOTE: "THEY HAVEN'T GOTTEN ME YET." HE SAID THEY VAPORIZED A WHOLE VILLAGE BUT THEY DIDN'T GET THE DINKS BECAUSE THEY GO DOWN TUNNELS. THERE'S 200 MILES OF TUNNELS. AGNER SAYS YOU JUST DROP A GRENADE IN AND LET IT ROLL. I ASKED CINDY WHO GOT VAPORIZED IF IT WASN'T THE DINKS.

SAY PEACE AND RIGHT ON.

SAY IT.

YOU HAVE TO SAY IT.

AGNER SAID A PLATOON GOT BLOWN UP BY OUR OWN PLANES AND THE GUYS IN THE PLATOON STARTED SHOOTING BACK. I GUESS WAR IS CATCHING. ALSO AGNER SAYS FOR ME TO QUIT WRITING HIS BUDDY MIKE ALL THAT PEACE CRAP. TO SAVE IT FOR THE HIPPIES. AND THAT DINKS ARE NOT PEOPLE. AGNER DOESN'T THINK OF DINKS AS PEOPLE.

OK, YOU SAY PEACE AND I SAY RIGHT ON. OK? GET IT?

PEACE.

RIGHT ON!

TO HIM THEY'RE JUST SOMETHING YOU SHOOT. CINDY'S DAD THINKS THEY'RE JUST SOMETHING YOU BOMB. OUR PRESIDENT AGREES. CINDY SAYS IT'S SAD AND ALL BUT IT'S NOT LIKE WE'RE BOMBING A PLACE ANYONE WAS PLANNING THEIR VACATIONS EVER. SHE SAYS AT LEAST THE WAR ISN'T IN CALIFORNIA OR HAWAII. "JUST THINK OF HOW BAD IT WOULD BE THEN"

PEACE.

RIGHT ON!

PEACE

RIGHT ON!

PEACE

RIGHT ON!!

WORKED UP

BY LYNDA "GEORGE + SADDAM = TRUE LOVE" BARRY © 91

WAR! UH! GOOD GOD Y'ALL! WHAT IS IT GOOD FOR! MY SISTER MARLYS KEPT SINGING THAT SONG AT RECESS. HER TEACHER SAID STOP. MARLYS SAID IT'S A FREE COUNTRY. HER TEACHER CALLED OUR GRANDMA. IT IS NOT A FREE COUNTRY FOR MARLYS ANY MORE.

OR ME. OUR GRANDMA SAID MARLYS WOULDN'T BE SO WORKED UP ABOUT THE WAR IF IT WASN'T FOR ME. WE GOT A NEW RULE AT OUR HOUSE. NO TALKING ABOUT IT. IF IT COMES ON THE TV, TURN IT OFF. IF YOU WANT TO TALK ABOUT WAR THEN GO OVER TO MR. LUDERMYER'S WHO SAYS JUST BOMB THEM ALL AND LET GOD SORT THEM OUT LATER.

LAST NIGHT MARLYS WOKE ME UP TO SAY HER DREAM. IT WAS THAT ALL THE PEOPLE WHO GOT BOMBED WENT INTO THE MATTRESS OF THE PRESIDENT. SHE SAID HIS BED WAS VERY HIGH. I THINK THE DREAM WAS FROM THAT STORY "THE PRINCESS AND THE PEA." DIFFERENCE WAS THOUGH, THE PRESIDENT COULD SLEEP.

MY GRANDMA SAYS THERE'S NOT A DAMN THING I CAN DO ABOUT THE WAR. BUT SHE IS WRONG. I CAN YELL STOP. I CAN SHOUT IT AND SAY IT AND WRITE IT AND THINK IT. I WANT TO BE <u>THE EVIDENCE</u> THAT NOT EVERYONE HERE SAID IT'S OK TO KILL THE PEOPLE THERE. NOT EVERYONE HERE THINKS AMERICANS COUNT MORE TO GOD. IN MY BEDROOM MY PRAYER IS SILENT NIGHT NO BOMBS. HOLY NIGHT NO KILLING. ALL IS CALM PEACE.

A GOOD CAUSE

BY LYNDA "100 HOURS" BARRY ✿ © 1991

I KNOW WHY PEOPLE THINK OF HEAVEN. WHEN YOU DIE YOU'RE GOING TO WANT SOME PLACE TO GO. ONE THING I DON'T KNOW: SAY IF YOU DIED BECAUSE SOMEONE KILLED YOU. THEN LATER ON THEY COME UP TO HEAVEN TOO. WHAT DO YOU SAY WHEN YOU SEE EACH OTHER?

WHAT IT IS, SOUL SISTER.

THERE'S AN IDEA THAT IF SOMEONE KILLS YOU THEY COULD NEVER GET IN HEAVEN ANYWAY, EXCEPT IF THEY KILLED YOU IN A WAR, THEN THEY GET AN EXCUSE SLIP FROM THE PRESIDENT.

ARE YOU RIDING ON A BUMMER?

KINDA

WANT TO HEAR MY POETRY?

THE EXCUSE SAYS NO OFFENSE BECAUSE IT WAS NOTHING PERSONAL. NOTHING TO DO WITH YOUR PERSONALITY OR ANYTHING. JUST MY PRESIDENT HATED YOUR PRESIDENT SO EXCUSE ME BUT HERE'S A BOMB. IN HEAVEN PEOPLE ARE MORE UNDERSTANDING ABOUT THIS THAN DOWN HERE.

THREE SIX NINE YOUR MAMA DRANK WINE. I PSYCHED YOUR MIND OUT TWENTY FIVE TIMES.

I KNOW WHY PEOPLE THINK OF HEAVEN. A PLACE WHERE MEN WOMEN AND CHILDREN AND EVEN THEIR PETS WILL COME UP TO YOU AND SAY IT'S OK YOU KILLED ME. I HEARD IT WAS FOR A VERY GOOD CAUSE.

POETRY'S NICE, HUH?

IT RELAXES YOUR BRAINS.

new years is coming what are your resolutions by Marlys!

① don't go cutting your friends hair without asking their mom first.

OH NO! You are bald headed! who did it?

marlys

② don't feed a dog a whole old pack of baloney.

who fed you it?

marlys BARF

③ don't tell people you can control bees with your mind.

you got 15 stings who told you it was ok to pet bees?

marlys

④ Don't pour milk in Donny Bauers trumpet or put food in it. Leave Donny Bauers trumpet alone even if you hate him and even if it's just sitting there and you think no ones watching

MARLYS!

← the smell remains

YOU ARE LEAVING

BY LYNDA "KONI KONI NUKI HOWHOW" BARRY © 1991

MOM WANTS US BACK. IT'S FOR SURE AND IT'S FOR REAL AND YOU WANT TO KNOW THE BEST PART? I THINK SHE THINKS WE'RE SUPPOSED TO BE HAPPY ABOUT IT. THAT'S SO FUNNY I FORGOT TO LAUGH.

termites by Marlys Mullen
Unit 2 Insects p. 37-39.
Termites

They can eat wooden shelves and books the whole library and do much damage. Things fall apart when they come.

The queen she just lays there.

ME, MARLYS AND FREDDY ARE SUPPOSED TO JUST FORGET OUR LIVES AT GRANDMAS, JUST FORGET OUR FRIENDS, AND OUR SCHOOL, AND KABAM! JUST GO BACK TO LIVING WITH MOM. KABAM! JUST BECAUSE SHE SAYS NOW SHE WANTS US. AND MY GRANDMA SAYS THERE IS NOTHING SHE CAN DO.

 the eggs

the queen can lay thousands in a day.

the eggs grow into:

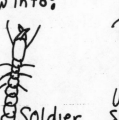

Worker   Soldier   Winged Swarmer

SHE THINKS MOM GOT LONELY. IS THAT MY PROBLEM? WHEN I TURN 18, WHEN I TURN 18, WHEN I TURN 18, WON'T BE NOBODY TELLING ME WHAT TO DO. GOING TO GET IN A CAR AND MAN, JUST FLOOR IT! GRANDMA COULD SAY NO. SHE COULD SAY NO NO NO HELL NO. BUT INSTEAD SHE SAYS SATURDAY. ON SATURDAY YOU ARE LEAVING.

they eat wood but cannot digest it actually. theres one celled animals in their guts that digest it. IF the one CELL things die the termite starves.

OOH NO

My buddy is dead

So what keep working

THE JOKE IS HOW. MOM IS TOO NERVOUS TO DRIVE US, GRANDMA IS TOO OLD, NO ONE KNOWS WHERE DAD IS AND UNCLE JOHN IS A QUEER WHICH DOES NOT AFFECT YOUR DRIVING BUT MY GRANDMA WON'T EVEN LET US SAY HIS NAME. SO WHAT IS THE CHOICE? ARE YOU READY ITS THE BUS. I'M OLD ENOUGH THEY TELL ME. I'M OLD ENOUGH TO TAKE US ACROSS 3 DAYS AND 2 NIGHTS. THEY TELL ME I ALWAYS WAS VERY OLD FOR MY AGE.

they live inside wooden things a long time then the wooden thing Falls over wrecked up. Then they move. Termite is not my first pick if I Got to be an insect.

Here we

GO

AGAIN

GET GOING

BY LYNDA "JUMP IN A VOLCANO" BARRY © 1992

IT'S SNOWING NOW. OUT MY WINDOW I CAN SEE IT FALLING BY THE STREETLIGHT. AT MY MOMS THERE'S HARLDLY EVER SNOW. MOSTLY JUST RAIN, RAIN, RAIN. ME AND MARLYS AND FREDDY GET ON THE BUS TOMORROW, THEN AFTERWARDS WE GET OFF AND WE'LL BE LIVING WITH GOOD OLD MOM AGAIN.

I'M LEAVING MY GOOD OLD SCHOOL HERE AND MY GOOD OLD FRIENDS HERE AND MY WHOLE GOOD OLD LIFE HERE JUST BECAUSE SHE WANTS US BACK NOW. WHY? I HEARD MRS. LUDERMYER SAY BECAUSE MY MOTHER WANTS A HOUSEKEEPER. SUPPOSED TO BE ME. I DOUBT THAT THOUGH. MY MOMS MAIN THING IN LIFE IS CLEANING. SHE NEVER THOUGHT I DID IT GOOD.

GOOD OLD MOM. WONDER WHY SHE WANTS US BACK. I AM SERIOUS. I DO NOT KNOW. ALL I KNOW IS WE GOT OUR THINGS PACKED AND GRANDMA CALLED THE BUS TO ASK SPECIAL PERMISSION, SHE LIED AND SAID I WAS 16, CAN A 16 YEAR OLD TAKE HER BROTHER AND SISTER ON A BUS THREE DAYS ALONE? AND THE GOOD OLD ANSWER IS YES.

SO HERE GOES. IF YOU LOOK AT THE LIGHTED DIAL ON THE CLOCK YOU'LL SEE THAT BUS LEAVES IN 5 MORE HOURS AND I'VE JUST BEEN LAYING HERE AND LAYING HERE. EVERYONE'S ASLEEP BUT ME. JUST LAYING HERE WATCHING THE DINKY RED HAND MOVING IN CIRCLES. MOVING UNTIL MY GOOD OLD GRANDMA SHOUTS UP THE STAIRS "WAKE UP KIDS! IT'S TIME TO GET GOING!"

I WILL BET YOU

By LYNDA "TICKET IN MY HAND" BARRY © 1992

FREDDY GETS THE WINDOW I GET THE AISLE MARLYS GETS THE OTHER WINDOW AND A FAT LADY IS SITTING BESIDE MARLYS AND MARLYS SAID ARE YOU GOING TO HAVE A BABY? AND THE LADY SAID "GOOD GOD NO HONEY THATS ALL ME HA-HA" AND SHE LOOKS AROUND AT THE OTHER BUS PASSENGERS.

"HA-HA" SHE SAYS AND ASKS MARLYS WHERE SHE'S GOING AND MARLYS BLABS HER ENTIRE LIFE STORY PLUS MY ENTIRE LIFE STORY PLUS OUR MOMS. SHE TELLS THE FAT LADY HOW MOM DITCHED US BUT NOW WANTS US BACK BUT SHE DOESN'T SAY DITCHED. THAT'S MY WORD. AT THE FIRST STOP THE FAT LADY BUYS MARLYS A CANDY NECKLACE ON AN ELASTIC STRING.

"I BET YOUR MAMA IS GOING TO BE SO HAPPY TO SEE You." SAYS THE FAT LADY AND MARLYS SAYS YES. MARLYS SAYS SHE WOULD BET HER FIVE DOLLARS THAT MOM WILL BE HAPPY. THEN SHE SHOWS THE FAT LADY HER FIVE DOLLAR BILL SHE GOT FROM GRANDMA. FREDDY ISN'T TALKING. "HOW ARE YOU FREDDY?" I SAY. "I AM FINE" SAYS FREDDY.

HE FINALLY SAYS HE WANTS TO SIT WITH MARLYS. TWO KIDS IN ONE SEAT BY THE FAT LADY AND RIGHT NOW THEY ARE ALL ASLEEP. FREDDY IN THE MIDDLE LEANING ON THE LADY WHO SAID 50 MILLION TIMES "I WOULD GIVE ANYTHING IN THE WORLD TO HAVE KIDS LIKE YOU." PLEASE GOD LET IT BE TRUE. WHEN WE GET OFF THIS BUS PLEASE GOD LET MOM BE HAPPY TO SEE US.

GOD'S BLESSING.

BY LYNDA "PASS ME THAT BOILED EGG" BARRY © 1992

THE FAT LADY GOT OFF THE BUS IN SPOKANE. SHE HUGGED MARLYS. SHE HUGGED FREDDIE. SHE TOLD ME I HAD TO EAT MORE AND IMPROVE MY ATTITUDE IN LIFE. SHE SAID A FAMILY COMING BACK TOGETHER WAS A SIGN OF GOD'S BLESSING.

SHE SAID SHE ALWAYS WANTED CHILDREN BUT COULDN'T HAVE THEM. MOM SAID SHE NEVER WANTED CHILDREN BUT SHE HAD THREE. I TAKE THAT BACK. MOM SAYS SHE WANTS US NOW. THAT'S WHY THIS LONG BUS RIDE THAT'S WHY I JUST THREW UP THE BARBEQUE POTATO CHIPS AND MILK I HAD FOR BREAKFAST. PEOPLE SAY GIRLS THROW UP FOOD BECAUSE THEY'RE SCARED OF GETTING FAT. THAT'S NOT WHY I DO IT.

THE BUS DRIVER JUST SAID WE WILL BE THERE IN 15 MORE MINUTES. IS MOM ALREADY AT THE BUS STATION WAITING? SHE TOLD MARLYS ON THE TELEPHONE THAT SHE GOT A DOG. NAME IS BABY. A FOX TERRIER GIRL. WILL BABY BE IN THE CAR? WILL MOM HAVE A SCARF ON AND WILL SHE BE SMOKING A WINSTON AND WILL SHE KNOW US RIGHT AWAY? DEAR MOM SOMETIMES I HAVE MISSED YOU VERY BAD.

"I SAW HER CAR!" SHOUTS MARLYS. "I SAW IT!" WE'RE ABOUT TO TURN INTO THE STATION AND IT IS, IT IS MOM'S CAR HER SAME CAR, THE DRIVER PUSHES THE GAS AND TURNS THE WHEEL, BUMP UP THE DRIVEWAY AND "MOM!" THE SHOUT OF "MOM! MOM! MOM!" WHEN WE SEE HER JUMPING THEN WAVING AND THEN RUNNING TO THE BUS DOOR. MOM. MOM. BEAUTIFUL BEAUTIFUL MOM.

THE WAY BACK

BY LYNDA "WAY DOWN YONDER IN NEW ORLEANS" BARRY

I'M ALL THE WAY BACK HOME NOW. GOT MY SAME ROOM, GOT MY SAME MOM, GOT A NEW DOG, A GREAT DOG, NAMED BABY. PLEASE DON'T THINK THIS NEXT PART IS WEIRD BECAUSE YOU COULD IF YOU DIDN'T KNOW MY MOM: SHE SAID IT WAS BECAUSE OF BABY SHE WANTED US BACK.

SHE SAID ONE DAY SHE WAS LOOKING AT BABY AND BABY LOOKED SO LONELY THAT MOM REALIZED HAVING KIDS AROUND TO PLAY WITH WOULD MAKE BABY HAPPY SO THAT'S WHEN SHE CALLED GRANDMA AND SAID "GIVE ME MY CHILDREN BACK." BUT MOM MEANS THAT STORY AS A JOKE. SHE LAUGHED AFTER SHE TOLD IT THEN WE LAUGHED THEN MOM POINTED OUT HOW I GOT BOSEMS.

SHE SAID I WAS DEVELOPING AND I SAID COULD WE TALK ABOUT IT LATER AND SHE SAID YES WE NEEDED TO HAVE A PRIVATE TALK AND WHEN MARLYS AND FREDDY WENT TO SLEEP, IN FRONT OF JOHNNY CARSON WE HAD IT. SHE ASKED ME DID I KNOW ABOUT THE CENSORED CENSORED CENSORED THINGS IN LIFE AND I SAID I DID. "WHERE'D YOU LEARN IT?" I SAID "IN HEALTH." I KNOW IT'S A LIE BUT I WASN'T ABOUT TO SAY "FROM DOUG."

WHO IS DOUG ANYWAY ANY MORE? HE WAS IN MY OLD LIFE. NOW I GOT A BRAND NEW ONE. NOW THAT I MOVED BACK HERE THE STORY OF MY LIFE IS WASHED WHITER THAN SNOW BECAUSE NO ONE KNOWS ANYTHING ABOUT ME. MOM SAYS I DON'T HAVE TO START MY NEW SCHOOL UNTIL MONDAY. THAT GIVES ME FIVE DAYS TO EXPERIMENT ON MY NEW PERSONALITY: SHY. DEEP. STRAIGHT A's. AND A BRITISH ACCENT.

SUPER RIGHT ON!

BY LYNDA "CHECK OUT JOHN MOONEY ON ROUNDER" BARRY © 92

Here's a incredible list of RightOns by my family! You should also ask your family for a list of their RIGHT ons! Everyone should tell their Right ons! What's your right ons?

Oh yeah say RIGHT ON!!! | by *Marlys* | Right on | right on hand

My Mom's Right Ons:

Lysol liquid + spray!

Chances Are

Johnny Mathis!

WOOLITE

MR. Clean

SALVO

PINESOL

Formula 409

Shell no pest strips

SLUG BAIT

WIN-STONS

The WHITE Tornado AJAX

rubber gloves

Freddie's RIGHT ONS:

His pet fly name of JEFF!

The Parts of a insect leg! (he said I had to put it in)

trochanter   Femer   tibia   tarsus

tweezers!

The song called psychotic reaction BY THE COUNT FIVE

Please Don't Bug me I just Croaked (my joke!) Haha

Giant Water Bug Because it can pretend its dead for around 15 minutes.

SLUG BAIT

THROWING AWAY THE SLUG BAIT + no pest strip

Jars with holes in the lid + dirt in the Bottom

His SECRET UNDER WEAR DANCING TO THAT SONG

Pulvilli. he said thats What insects Use to walk on glass + the Ceiling. He said he wants it on his feet. RIGHT ON PULVILLI!

LUCKY Glow in the dark Light Bulb 1¢ PRIZES from Gum machines

GOING INTO OUTER Space to investigate if there's insects in or ter space

Maybonnes Right ons:

EQUALITY!

peace!

Donovan!

nair nair!

Her diary!

FROSTED CHERRY LIPSTICK!

ecology

Astrology + ESP

the song, Groovin' By Tommy James and the Shondells

Incredible FLOWER POWER Bell bottoms that mom won't Let her wear. But she sneaks them sometimes.

Once she asked our mom the names of The Beatles and mom said
1. CURLEY
2. MOE
3. ROGER
4. SWIRLEY.

Maybonne says thats her FUNNY RIGHT on!

Theres more But now she says for me to QUIT BUGGING HER SO FORGET HER THEN! FINE!!

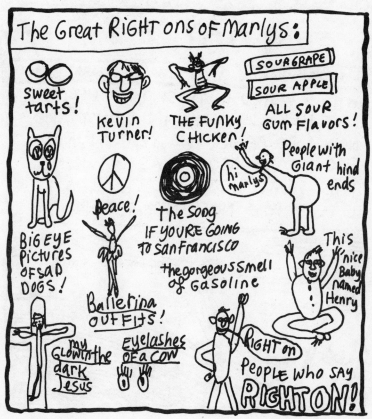

The Great RIGHT ons of Marlys:

sweet tarts!

Kevin Turner!

THE FUNKY CHICKEN!

SOURGRAPE SOUR APPLE ALL SOUR GUM Flavors!

People with Giant hind ends

hi marlys

Big EYE Pictures of SAD DOGS!

peace!

Ballerina OUTFITS!

the song IF YOU'RE GOING to San Francisco

the gorgeous smell of Gasoline

This nice Baby named Henry

my GLOW in the dark Jesus

Eyelashes of a cow

RIGHT on

PEOPLE WHO SAY RIGHT ON!

MAY I?

LYNDA "YOU WILL SEE THE ZULU KING" BARRY © 1992

WHAT'S WEIRD IS THIS: OK. I <u>USED</u> TO LIVE HERE AND THEN I DIDN'T AND NOW I DO AGAIN TWO YEARS LATER. TWO YEARS AGO I WAS WALKING THIS SAME EXACT HILL TO SCHOOL LIKE IT WAS NOTHING. BUT NOW?

NOW IT'S LIKE I'M WALKING IN A MOVIE. LIKE I'M FLAT ON THE SCREEN OF THE MOVIE OF MY LIFE. HERE'S THE PART OF ME WALKING TO SCHOOL, FIRST DAY AT MY OLD SCHOOL AND DIFFERENT PEOPLE STARING AT MY HEAD LIKE I'M A RE-RUN OF MYSELF. A GHOST. NOT EVEN SURE SHOULD THEY SAY MY NAME.

I KNOW. IT DOESN'T SEEM REAL EVEN TO ME. I KNOW ALL THE FACES AND THEY KNOW ME BUT THE REALITY IS NOBODY KNOWS ANYTHING YET. THOSE TWO YEARS ARE LIKE TWO BOOKS MISSING OUT OF MY ENCYCLOPEDIA. CAN'T NOBODY DO A REPORT ON THOSE TWO YEARS UNLESS I OPEN MY MOUTH.

SO THAT'S WHY I'M NOT SAYING A WORD UNTIL I FIND BRENDA. MY BEST FRIEND OF TWO YEARS AGO. I'VE BEEN IN A PLAN TO SUR-PRISE HER BECAUSE SHE DOESN'T KNOW I'M BACK. I'VE BEEN PRAC-TICING MY FIRST THING I'LL SAY: "EXCUSE ME, MAY I BLOW YOUR MIND?"

MAYBONNE!!

MY BAD ASS LIFE

By Lynda • "Read Confederacy of Dunces" Barry ©1992

WHAT IS BRENDA'S TRIP? I TRIED TO BLOW HER MIND WITH THE SURPRISE OF ME MOVING BACK HERE AND NOW SHE'S BLOWING MINE BY ACTING SO FREAKY. FREAKY DEAKY. TELLING ME "PLEASE DON'T TELL NO ONE NOTHING ABOUT YOUR LIFE UNTIL LUNCH." OK. IT'S LUNCH.

ARE YOU A HOE?

I DON'T GET IT.

THEY SAID TO ME YOUR SISTER IS A HOE.

IT'S LUNCH AND I'M BY HER LOCKER BUT WHERE IS BRENDA? FIRST BELL. THEN SECOND BELL. FORGET IT. I'M STARVING AND I'M EATING. SO I GO INTO THE LUNCHROOM, RIGHT? AND THERE SHE IS, THERE'S BRENDA, SITTING WITH THE GIRLS FROM THE VIEW AND I'M WALKING UP TO HER ALL " WHAT GIVES?" AND SHE JUMPS UP LIKE SHE'S JUST BEEN BUSTED SHOPLIFTING.

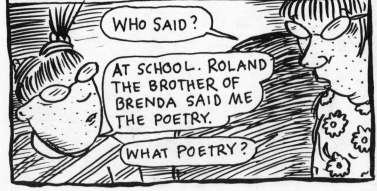

WHO SAID?

AT SCHOOL. ROLAND THE BROTHER OF BRENDA SAID ME THE POETRY.

WHAT POETRY?

ALL THE GIRLS AT HER TABLE STOP EATING, STOP TALKING, STOP <u>EVERYTHING</u>, AND LOOK AT ME LIKE I'M THE NEW NATIONAL ATTENTION THEN BRENDA HOOKS ME BY THE ARM AND STARTS DRAGGING ME TO THE CAN. WHAT, GIVES BRENDA, WHAT GIVES? SHE'S SO FREAKED OUT SHE DRAGS ME INTO THE <u>BLACK</u> GIRLS CAN AND THEY STARE AND BRENDA PUTS US BOTH IN A STALL AND SHUTS THE DOOR. "WHAT?" I GO, "<u>WHAT?</u>"

TICK TACK TOE YOUR SISTER IS A HOE.

STREETWALKER HOE. ARE YOU IT?

THAT BRENDA.

I'M HEARING "LESBIAN!" I HEAR "HEY LESBO!" AND BRENDA IS CRYING AND TELLING ME NOT TO WRECK HER LIFE AND THAT SHE'S SORRY SHE'S SORRY FOR, <u>GET THIS</u>, ALL THE LIES SHE'S BEEN TELLING PEOPLE ABOUT MY LIFE. MADE UP STORIES. LIES ABOUT WHAT MY LETTERS SAID. SHE MADE UP A BAD ASS LIFE FOR ME. AND NOW SHE'S BEGGING ME NOT TO BUST HER TO THE VIEW GIRLS WHO ARE <u>HER</u> LIFE. WHAT SHOULD I DO?

TRUE OR FALSE?

FALSE.

OK I'LL KICK ROLAND'S HINDER FOR YOU THEN.

The Liar and the Ho

BY LYNDA "HI MIKE ROCHELEAU" BARRY © 1992

BRENDA SAID TO ME PLEASE TRY TO UNDER-STAND WHY SHE MADE UP THE STORIES ABOUT ME BEING A RUNAWAY STREET-WALKING HO. TELLING PEOPLE MY AD-VENTURES LIKE I WAS AN X-RATED PER-SON. SHE SAID IT WAS ALL IN MY LETTERS TO HER WHICH <u>SHE</u> WROTE <u>HERSELF.</u>

BRENDA BEGGING ME NOT TO BUST HER ON HER LIES BUT I AM IN FAVOR OF REALNESS ABOUT WHO YOU ARE AND I AM <u>NOT</u> A RUNAWAY STREET WALKING HO. I'M SORRY BRENDA BUT YOU'RE LYING. BRENDA SAYS "AM <u>NOT.</u>" IN FRONT OF HER FRIENDS FROM THE VIEW. I SAY "ARE <u>TOO.</u>" IN FRONT OF THE SAME VIEW GIRLS. WE SAY IT OVER AND OVER UNTIL WE SHOUT IT.

122

AND I CAN SEE THE VIEW GIRLS DOUBTING BRENDA THEN DOUBTING ME THEN DOUBTING BRENDA UNTIL THEY DECIDE TO BELIEVE US BOTH. THAT BRENDA IS A LIAR AND I AM A HO. I TELL THEM IT DOESN'T MAKE SENSE TO BELIEVE TWO OPPOSITE THINGS BUT THEY LIKE HAVING A HO AND A LIAR AROUND THE SCHOOL. TO TALK ABOUT AND THINK ABOUT AND IGNORE IN THE HALL.

SO NOW THE LIAR IS OUT AND THE HO IS OUT AND THAT'S HOW ME AND BRENDA GOT BACK TOGETHER. AND HOW WE GOT OUR REPUTATIONS. AND INVITED TO PARTIES THIS WEEK-END OF GUYS MOSTLY GUYS. BRENDA ASKED ME DO I HATE HER FOR IT AND I SAID NOT IF THESE PARTIES TURN OUT FUN.

OK BUT DON'T YOU NEVER TELL NO LIES ON ME AGAIN.

SWEAR.

123

OUR·INCREDIBLE·PARTY

BY LYNDA "GO SEE HOME and AWAY" BARRY © 1992

THE PARTY OF MOSTLY ALL GUYS, I DON'T ACTUALLY KNOW HOW IT TURNED OUT BECAUSE IT WAS ALREADY BEING BUSTED BY THE POLICE WHEN WE GOT THERE. I GUESS THEY HAD A KEG. WE WATCHED FROM BEHIND THIS LADY'S BUSHES AND THEN SHE TURNED THE <u>HOSE ON US!</u>

YOU DRANK WINE.

DON'T TALK TO ME.

AND DON'T MOVE THE BED.

ME, BRENDA, AND HER COUSIN THE DRAG GO RUNNING INTO THE STREET. THE DRAG IS SCREAMING SHE WANTS TO GO HOME SO BRENDA SCREAMS BACK "THEN <u>GO!</u>" BUT THE DRAG WON'T GO WITHOUT BRENDA, I GUESS BECAUSE THEY ARE COUSINS. BRENDA SAYS HAVING A COUSIN LIKE THE DRAG IS A CURSE ON HER LIFE. BUT TRUTHFULLY, I WANTED TO GO HOME TOO. BUT WE HAD ALREADY GOTTEN THE WINE.

YOU'RE A JUVENILE DELINQUINT.

MARLYS SHUT UP.

MOM'S MAD.

SCORED **3** BOONES FARM APPLE WINES BY BRENDA ASKING DIFFERENT GUYS WOULD THEY BUY IT FOR HER. IN FRONT OF THE STORE SHE ASKED ALL GUYS WITH BEARDS. FINALLY ONE GUY DID. YOU CAN SAY BRENDA IS BOLD. ALSO YOU CAN SAY WE GOT SO DRUNK THAT EVERY ONE OF US THREW UP. BRENDA WANTED TO BARF IN THE YARD OF THE LADY OF THE GARDEN HOSE BUT DIDN'T MAKE IT.

SHE SAID SHE'LL SEND YOU BACK TO GRANDMAS.

NO SHE WON'T.

NO WAY COULD WE GO HOME SO WE WENT TO THE GRADE SCHOOL AND LAID DOWN ON THE HILL BEHIND ONE OF THE PORTABLES. THE DRAG, BRENDA, AND ME, ALL OF US LOOKING UP AT THE NIGHT OF STARS AND BREATHING AS MUCH AIR AS WE COULD. AIR AIR AIR. WAITING UNTIL WE COULD WALK STRAIGHT AND TALK STRAIGHT SO WE COULD ALL GO HOME AND GET SCREAMED AT BY OUR MOMS AND THEN LAY IN BED AND SWEAR WE WILL NEVER DO IT AGAIN.

NOW I LAY ME DOWN TO SLEEP I'M SORRY GOD BUT MY SISTERS A WINO.

SHUT UP MARLYS.

N·O·MATTER·WHAT

BY LYNDA "BLACKBIRD SINGING" BARRY © 1998

ANOTHER SCHOOL PSYCHOLOGICAL LADY SHOWED UP TODAY AND WHO SHE WANTED TO SEE WAS ME AND BRENDA AND IF BRENDA'S COUSIN THE DRAG WAS THERE SHE WOULD HAVE WANTED TO SEE HER TOO BECAUSE WORD GOT OUT ABOUT US BEING DRUNK. SHE SAID "DRAW PICTURES OF YOUR FAMILY DOING SOMETHING"

I SAID "I ALREADY DID THAT ONE BEFORE." SHE SAID WELL, DO IT AGAIN AND THAT ME AND BRENDA WERE SKATING ON THIN ICE AND DUH, DUH, DUH. THEN SHE GETS MAD BECAUSE THAT'S WHAT I DRAW A PICTURE OF BUT TRUTHFULLY IT DOES FIT. SEEMS LIKE THE WHOLE WORLD IS SKATING ON THIN ICE BUT AT LEAST WE'RE SKATING.

SHE MADE BRENDA LEAVE AND THEN
TOLD ME I WAS DRAGGING BRENDA
DOWN TO MY LEVEL SHE SAID SHE HAD
HEARD ALL ABOUT ME I SAID THAT WAS
LIES MADE UP BY BRENDA SHE SAID
COWARDS ALWAYS BLAME SOMEONE
ELSE AND ASKED ME IF SHE SHOULD
CALL MY MOM AND I SAID PLEASE DON'T
CALL MY MOM AND SHE SAID "I WON'T"
THEN SHE CALLED MY MOM.

THAT'S WHY I'M ON RESTRICTION NOW FOR
LIFE AND THAT'S WHY I SNEAK OUT
MY BEDROOM WINDOW AT NIGHT, IN
THE MIDDLE OF THE NIGHT, AND CLIMB
ON THE ROOF OF MY OLD GRADE SCHOOL
AND JUST SIT IN THE PEACE AND QUIET
OF THE DARK. THE GREAT PEACE AND
QUIET WHERE I CAN PRAY FOR THINGS
TO TURN OUT ALL RIGHT EVEN THOUGH I
CAN'T STOP BREAKING ALL THE RULES.
AND I PRAY TO KEEP ON BELIEVING LIFE
IS MAGICAL NO MATTER WHAT, THAT IS MY
MAIN GOAL IN LIFE, DEAR GOD SWEAR TO
GOD I WILL KEEP ON BELIEVING IT'S MAGIC
IT'S MAGIC IT'S **STILL SO MAGIC**

HEY!

FOUND YA!

HELP ME
UP, OK?